THIS OTHER BREED -EAST ANGLIANS

BY MICHAEL WATKINS

EAST ANGLIAN MAGAZINE LIMITED IPSWICH SUFFOLK

I.S.B.N. 0 900227 35 4

Printed and published in England by
East Anglian Magazine Ltd
6 Great Colman Street
Ipswich, Suffolk.
© East Anglian Magazine Ltd 1978
Cover drawing 'Suffolk Haymakers' by
Harry Becker, in the possession of the author.
Cover design by Lynn Sheridan.

CONTENTS

	Introduction	5
1.	The Horseman	11
2.	The Village Schoolteacher	17
3.	The Law	22
4.	The Verger	30
5.	The Lifeboat Coxwain	36
6.	The G.P.	41
7.	The Stranger	48
8.	The Journalist	53
9.	The Blind Man	60
10.	The Trawlerman	66
11.	The Parson	70
12.	The Landowner	77
13.	The Media Man	85
14.	The Shopkeeper	91
15.	The Factory Worker	96
16.	The Meals-on-Wheels Helper	101
17.	The Commuter	107
18.	The Blacksmith	113
19.	The Publican	118
20.	The Nun	123
21.	The Sportsman	129
22.	The Nurse	135
23.	The Weekenders	141
24.	The School Leaver	146
25.	The Baker	150
26.	The Gravedigger	155

*For
Nell Bloor,
one of the breed*

This Other Breed — Introduction

SEVENTEEN YEARS ago I was a nomad. My tent had been pitched in London and in New York, it had been pitched in Singapore; at one time it had been pitched, quite literally, in the Malaysian jungle, little distance from the township of Kuala Khubu Bharu. By my middle 20's I had become as footloose, as disoriented — geographically and emotionally — as the hippies of today. And what I had seen of the world I did not altogether care for.

It seemed to me that urban life was going wrong. There was a sickness; a new kind of plague was spreading. An early symptom was cynicism, which led men to cheat at work, then to cheat at home, and finally to cheat themselves. A word crept into the language: 'status'. What did it mean? The facile answer was that the urban conscience, sense of value — call it what you will — was being manipulated. Like Pavlov's dog, we were learning tricks which, although not in our nature, were becoming second nature.

Lesson one was 'Dog eat dog'. At first a little shocking, this form of social cannibalism was soon to be a way of life. We saw it in the High Street the moment the supermarket opened its doors, offering twopence off our breakfast cereal. The corner shop, the one we had dealt with for years, could not compete; and thus could not survive. So there was a bright lick of paint along the High Street, and the kiss of death to all we had known.

It was a beginning. Nothing dramatic, no revolution; it was handled discreetly, smoothly, humanely. There were no screams, only whimpers, as independent names became, as if by massive deed-poll, corporate titles. And, you had to admit, it was nice to get twopence off the cornflakes. We had been made an offer we couldn't refuse.

In 1961 I was made a personal offer. It involved a large salary, working for an organisation for which I had no respect. It was symptomatic of the times that I actually considered the offer, debating with myself whether the money would anaesthetise my own conscience. Eventually, I saw it as a warning, as a breathlessness before the coronary. So I thanked God, or whoever is in charge of these things, packed my bag and came to East Anglia.

It was not as simple as that, of course. The Cotswolds, for which I have always had an affection, could have been my destination; Pembrokeshire even. The London home-counties never stood a chance because they were in direct line of fire from the barrage I was trying to avoid. No doubt I could have been happy elsewhere; but something drew me to East Anglia and this is where I stayed. Basically, it had to do with mud.

Ask people about East Anglia's outstanding visual quality, and inevitably you will be told about the vast Constable skies. You can see the *whole* sky, it is said. To be truthful as much as controversial, I am not at all sure I want to see the whole sky. I like hills, towering forests, sprawling valleys. What struck me about this landscape was that there was such a lot of mud. It had different colours and hues, a variety of textures; it was heavy, adhesive, clinging to your boots, binding you to the soil. That's what I liked, the very feeling when I went walking that I was bound to the soil. It was this experience, more than any other, that told me I had come home.

I bought a cottage, more or less the first I saw, in the Suffolk village of Baylham. On Sunday I occasionally read the lesson in St Peter's Church, and I walked. One of my walks, over the Wilsons' land and past Ditch Wood, brought me close to a rambling house with a mellowed jumble of roofs and chimneys. It was an isolated spot, full of secrets and magic, enclosed by tall trees and a moat. No other house was in sight. It was called Tarston Hall.

Mentioned in the Domesday Book, Tarsen Manor, as it was then known, fell into ruins to be replaced by another dwelling built in 1546. This is where I live, alone. For by one of those extraordinary quirks which happen once in a lifetime, I became the owner of Tarston within a year of my disaffection from London. It is the coldest house in the county, draughty, inconvenient, haunted by a gentle, wilful ghost called Hannah — and all I have ever wanted.

It would be good to tell that I became self-sufficient, growing my own cabbages and so on; but such is not the case. As a gardener, I am a total failure. They say you should talk to plants and this I tried last year with the tomatoes; but they could not have liked my tone, because they sulked, ending up the size of peas. My neighbours are good to me, however: the Vanes supply me with eggs, lettuce, strawberries; and Mrs. Chaplin, when she was a mite younger than her 92 years, made me sausage rolls and elderberry wine. For the rest I shop at Young's in Needham Market, which is as independent a store as you will find: besides, Enid tends to spoil me.

My small successes are with wildlife, particularly the mallard who treat the moat as if they'd bought the lease. After months of quiet conversation, they came to eat out of my hand. I was proud of that. One tough old hen, Araminta I called her, became an especially close friend. Believe it or not, she used to meet my car as it turned through the gates, then she would walk me to the house. As I strolled about the garden she followed, a pace or two behind, squawking irritably if I went too fast. She would even come into the kitchen, chatting as I breakfasted; and when I went abroad, as I frequently do to gather material, I would return to a thinner, dejected Araminta. I am sure she pined.

One weekend I had an American archaeologist staying. She was playing with some children down by the water, while I was at my typewriter. Suddenly she came to me with tears in her eyes to say that the children had found Araminta dead in the moat. We were very upset, burying her beneath the old pear tree, next to the cat Domesday I inherited with the house.

In the country one is close to death; it is all around: young birds fall from nests, pheasants are taken by foxes, field mice by owls — so I suppose I am being sentimental when I say that I still miss Araminta.

Perhaps knowing an animal is easier than knowing a person; it requires less effort, less commitment. You can retain your privacy with animals as friends, giving as much of yourself as you wish and saying 'shoo' when you have had enough. Then I read Ronald Blythe's classic *Akenfield*, realising chapter by chapter that I was missing out on the men of Anglia; my seclusion had become inward-looking. So I started writing this book, trying to understand the people I had settled among.

Ronald Blythe and I have known one another a long while. Of *Akenfield* he once explained to me: 'My book was not intended to be anything more than a kind of autobiography in which I was re-hearing generations of my Suffolk rural background talking through the people living in and around Charsfield, where I lived for 20 years. It was also about the emergence of a critical voice — in the literary and artistic sense — from such a background.'

Anxious to see whether I was heading along the right lines, I sent Ronnie the first few chapters of *This Other Breed*. He replied: 'How excellently you have listened to the country people! And I particularly liked the way you have included the coastal people because they say something quite different to what is said in the interior.'

It was more than enough encouragement, and I went on to finish the book — a book about people, a race called East Anglians. All I had to do was listen. It is not my opinion that the East Anglian is better than his fellows; often he is less approachable, suspicious of innovation, not infrequently complacent. He will get to heaven no quicker than a Devonian or a Scot; all we may be sure of is that when he does arrive at his final destination he will be as cussed obstinate there as he is here. I hope that I shall be in his company, for it is a company I enjoy.

Readers should be warned that in two or three chapters I have disguised my subject and his location. This is so in the case of the doctor, both as a question of ethics, and to protect patients' relatives from distress. Neither should readers scour the map for Amos Legge's village of Deersthorpe, because it does not exist. Amos the Gravedigger exists — vociferously so — but I have given him another name and a fictitious address for reasons which will become apparent. The weekenders also have aliases because their views on East Anglians may prompt neighbours to heave bricks through the windows of their exquisite, part lived-in, part-loved rectory.

Certain London friends accuse me of turning my back on the vital issues of the day, of retreating to the peace of Tarston when I should be — figuratively speaking — carrying banners about inequality, injustice. To this I must plead guilty. My travels about the world have shown me much misery, much suffering. I have tried, in my newspaper and magazine articles and radio talks, to describe as honestly as I know how what I have seen. It is not enough and I am aware of this. But I am not a crusader; my armour is tarnished. I am a reporter, not a guerilla — and it is not in my nature to change at this stage of the game.

The countryside, East Anglia, will hold me. I have witnessed the terrible damage people do to one another, but I do believe that country folk are more gentle at heart than city dwellers. The plague has not annihilated them, and I trust it never will.

Yet the melancholy fact remains that city ways are catching on; some Suffolk lanes have become motorways. The old people in this book feel, on the whole, that yesterday made slightly better sense than today; and who can say with utter conviction that they are wrong? Take Katy the Recluse: her withdrawal marks a kind of wisdom. In Tom Woods' awful squalor there is a pride. And James the Horseman never did learn envy or distrust.

We should listen to the old people, for they have been where we have not. They have seen what we shall never see. They have heard the sound of silence. And when they go, things will never be quite the same. They are a dying breed. It is sad, but it is so.

MICHAEL WATKINS
NEEDHAM MARKET, SUFFOLK. 1978

The Horseman: James Welham

'DO YOU KNOW, there's not a single horse in this village today? There's no room for horses any more. I remember a world of silence... everything was horse-drawn, quiet as anything it was. None of these aeroplanes or cars, no television or wireless noise — just people talking to each other, and the sound of horses' hooves. People don't seem to speak to each other much today. Perhaps they don't like each other... it's the competition, everyone trying to be a bit better than the neighbours.

'No, I don't think I'd go on the land if I had my time over again. They ride everywhere, sitting up in tractors in their cabins, wearing those earphones, sitting up in combine harvesters. Sixteen men scything a cornfield, now that was a sight. That was something to look at... and children waiting for the rabbits to run out of the stubble.'

James Welham was born at Hintlesham in 1898, one of five boys and two girls. They lived near the George pub, in a red brick house, five brothers sleeping in one room, two sisters sleeping with the parents. Their father earned 13 shillings a week as a farm labourer, supplementing his income by odd-jobbing: gardening, timber felling, castrating pigs ('... he'd never touch a sow...'), sweet pickling bacon. The mother was Chapel, a 'fragile' woman who went blind after the Great War, dying at 60, to be joined by her husband when he was 85 years old.

'Father done well by us, I reckon. He was a bit of a scrounger as they'd say now — he knew where to pick up an old hare. We grew vegetables and made beer... he liked a pint. We'd eat well — meat pudding and dumplings, sheep's head, soup. No one went hungry. Father was a big man who knew the importance of feeding well. And we were always well shod; it was important to have strong boots, and there was lots that didn't. We always had good second-hand clothes as well, so we kept warm in winter... many families were worse off.'

The children went to the village school: 'We learnt

the three R's, but I wasn't all that keen. I wish now that I'd learnt more — I can see today that if you can read and write well you get a better job. I really started work when I was eight, chopping wood and milking cows before and after school. The farmer would give my mother a shilling a fortnight for that, and he gave me a good Saturday tea — bread and butter and cheese, cake . . . they'd really stuff me out.

'We left school at 13. Ruth, she went into service at Layham, John started with the horses, George became a cowman, Ned a stockman, Ben went on the land as well. Edith . . . well, when mother failed, Edith stayed at home to help out. They're all dead now — just me. My wife was one of eight, and she's the only one left too.'

At 80 James Welham seems fit enough, gardening in the village of Sproughton four half days a week, tending his own allotment as well. He stands straight, bending supply, his mind darting back 70 years or so without effort. There is no rancour in him, no resentment; his statement seems to be that his has been a good life and that there is still something to look forward to. Provided that he and his wife have each other, that they are not taken from one another.

Her name is Ada, 'plain Ada,' as she says, adding that it means 'happiness'. 'It'd be hard if one of us went,' she says. 'You've got to think about it, but it'd be hard on the one left.' Ada is as active as her husband, a tall, commanding looking woman with a sharp, direct look in her deep-set eyes. You can see why Jimmy, as she calls him, wed her on 11th March 1926; she must have been a dazzler, Ada the District Nurse, as she was then. 'He's been a kind husband,' she says. 'I won't say I didn't miss nursing, but with me kindness always came first. He's a good man and he's been a good husband.'

James started working full time for Mr. Ladbroke as back'us boy at Red House Farm, Hintlesham, cutting wood, lighting fires, cleaning stoves, from 6 am until 5.30 pm six days a week. No holidays, just Christmas Day and, because Mr. Ladbroke was a devout Chapel man, half a day on Good Friday.

'I went with the horses when I was 15. There was no alternative to horses, they did everything — ploughing, binding, cultivating, harrowing, carting to Ipswich. The war had come, you see, and men got short, they went off to fight old Fritz... then I went off myself, joined up with the Royal Fusiliers, a posh regiment.

'We went to France, to Étaples, then into the trenches at Arras. It was bad, very bad indeed. It's a mystery how any of us survived. Then we went to the front at Ypres and everything that happened before seemed like a school outing... we were called up there at two o'clock on a Sunday afternoon and Fritz gave us a real pasting. A lot of us got lost, we just wandered around for four days among the dead. You've never seen such dead – horses, men, you just rolled them aside and went on. The officers and N.C.O.'s were all killed, you see, there was no one to tell us what to do. Men just got blown apart and left there in the mud... you never forget that smell.

'The mud and the wet was the worst. You stood in water in the trenches, waiting. That was bad, the waiting. Men used to envy me because I could sleep. I could sleep anywhere, wet or dry, and we were never dry — so long as I had something to eat I could just sleep, even through gunfire.

'No, I wouldn't say I was scared. I was too young, I didn't really understand what it was all about. The older ones were frightened, the ones with wives and kids. Sometimes it was so bad you didn't mind if you did catch it — almost wanted to in a way. But when the roll was called and some of your mates didn't answer you felt sorry they'd gone. I caught this packet of gas then, we didn't see it at first — mucky stuff came up like a low ground mist. Had us coughing — coughing our lungs up and spewing. We marched into Germany then, 350 miles... I was lucky — after a time on Jankers, I got a cookhouse job. Came home after that... the Armistice. We'd won the war, you see.'

Sixty years on and he sees it all sharply, as if it were yesterday. They live, James and Ada, in a Sproughton council bungalow. Garden and house are neat, although Ada says the place is damp. There is a school playground behind so that they can see the children enjoying themselves. They like watching the young. They feel embarrassed about the garden next door: 'Said he'd cut his grass, but he never did...' The neglect offends them, bothers them as much as the international catastrophes they see on television. Ada loves music; preferring BBC2, but James cannot keep up with that so mostly they watch ITV.

As James talks, Ada listens to every word, happy in the reminiscences, caring as much for her husband, as affected by his kindness, as she was on the day they made their vows. There are photographs of the children: Bruce, retired from the police force, and June who married an airman from Bentwaters and flew the Atlantic to live in California. It is very beautiful in California, says Ada, although she has never been there. James sits on an upright chair at a table; he is a man not given to slouching. A clock ticks loudly, pressing in on the rare silences as James considers his memories.

'Came straight back to Hintlesham when the war ended, joined Mr. Warth as a full time horseman. Suffolks and Shires we had, big old horses, the Suffolks up to 20 hands, Shires a bit more. They'd weigh an awful lot 'cept when some old devils starved their horses. Suffolks had clean legs, not much hair — we didn't like them hairy horses, too much dirt on 'em. Had up to 20 horses. They were fed at 4 am, we'd be there at six, harness up and get out. We worked root crops, sugar beet, barley, wheat . . . everything those horses did.

'You coaxed 'em, you needed patience and you needed strength. Some were good workers; some would kick a town down to avoid work, they were that bad tempered. You could never tell until you got through to a horse — some might strike out with their forelegs or lash out with the back 'uns. There was a lot that got hurt. I got kicked on the knee once, that's all. There was some cruelty here and there, and that made animals vicious . . . suppose once or twice I might have used the stick when I shouldn't. The dealers were the worst ones, they'd beat the horses, tie 'em up.

'Once you got to know a horse you could do anything with him. They all had names . . . I had Captain, a big Suffolk, a real good nimble horse. We used to say a herky old horse wouldn't last long, they'd get exhausted. A lazy one you'd have to pay to work and that'd last 10 or 12 years before he'd ease up.

'Machinery started coming in during the 20's, for ploughing. I didn't think much of 'em . . . you'd get a hot shirt starting those first tractors, cranking up those old

Fergusons, then you'd get the shivers driving around in 'em. But horses lasted until the Second War. Farmers didn't care for tractors pressing the land down because they'd have to pull it up again. And men didn't take kindly to tractors — we were suspicious, I suppose. Mucky old things... dirty, with no mudguards, all noise and slushing wet. It changed when they put mudguards on. It took a young man to work with tractors... ones who didn't know horses. Your horse was a pal — you can't say that about tractors.

'There was bad feeling between horsemen and tractors. Tractors couldn't set square, they'd waste land not getting close to the headland. You got right up to it with a horse, but tractors took double the space, they couldn't turn well. They couldn't draw a straight furrow like a horse. Why, some horsemen could draw a furrow within quarter of an inch — you couldn't get a tractor doing that. The older men worried about that — it was our pride.'

Ada is not so sure about the pride of those days. She looks almost angry as she listens: 'I could see Jimmy ploughing from our cottage windows. Up and down, up and down, all day long, wet or dry. It never seemed to stop raining — he'd go out tied round with old sacks to keep the rain out and at night we'd try to dry them for the morning. It didn't seem fit work for a human being... it broke my heart to watch him. When he came off the land I thanked God.'

James Welham shakes his head mildly. He is not a man to make a fuss, to question the order of things. He was born to do as he was told, knowing his place; he was reared to duty and to acceptance. Spanish peasants of Old Castile are committed to a legend: 'We are born, we fight and we die.' That is all that matters. It is a chivalry James would understand; it has never occurred to him to do anything other than his duty. He has fought and has become one of the few survivors.

'Mr. Warth was a good master,' he says loyally, replying to his wife's bitterness. 'Sometimes, when we were sheep dipping, we'd work from 4 am till 9 pm and we'd be thankful that we were strong enough to do it. Ploughing wasn't so bad, you had something to hang on to, to lift your boots out of the mud. Harrowing and drilling was worse, but you were someone if you had a job. There was a lot of unemployment after the war. We lived in an age when we had nothing, so anything was good . . .

'No, I didn't feel let down after the trenches and the promises and all that. I don't think I was educated enough to think about right and wrong . . . we lived from day to day. It was a smaller world then — you learn about justice and what your rights are from television today. We know about countries I'd never heard of. I'm talking about long ago, when the important things were like keeping warm. If we had two rabbit dinners in a week, that was luxury.'

Ada says: 'Our daughter-in-law has bought us luxuries, a dryer and an electric blanket. We've never had a car . . . the idea! Our biggest luxury is that we're still together, we haven't been left alone. We're slowing up . . . I believe there's someone above and when it's time to go, we'll go.'

'Yes,' agrees James. 'The energy is going a bit . . . I'm getting like an old horse.'

The Village Schoolteacher: Joyce Cave

IN THE punishment book of Monks Eleigh School the first entry reads: 'Albert Head, aged 11. Offence: Continual disobedience. Nature of punishment: four cuts on hand. Date of punishment: 3 Oct. 1907.'

Then, in the hungry 20's the miscreant is Fred Buggs, aged nine. Offence: 'Taking turnips from Mr. Everitt and eating same. Two strokes on each hand (one extra for dodging). 18 May 1924.'

In the school log the headmistress writes on 24th April 1921: 'Am continuing fires in the infants' and other rooms in the morning as it is still very cold for young children. Summertime starts at school today.'

The log is still kept up to date, the punishment book abandoned in 1953 when, on 6th October, Richard Marsh received one stroke for the heinous crime of 'biting another boy'. The location for this act of cannibalism was in the old school building; it is something you would not expect in the new school, opened in 1961. And such a school it is, with vast windows opening on to rolling Suffolk meadows, its grass playing fields, its central heating and fully equipped kitchen. There is even a swimming pool for the 40 children, aged five to nine, to splash around in during the summer term: '... swimming is as much a curriculum activity as, say, reading or maths ...', states the school brochure prepared by headmistress, Joyce Cave.

The two classrooms are light and airy. 'Our dinosaur is as long as ... 14 chairs, 41 hands, 28 feet, 5 children ...', reads an illustrated notice. 'On Saturday we made a bird table; the first bird to come was a robin next came two bluetits ...', reads another. On the blackboard is chalked 'mr watkins is an author who has come to visit us to write about us in his new book. some capital letters are missing. can you find them?' In the corridor children's drawers are marked — Victoria Turner, Gavin Morris, Nicola Leeder ... and at nine o'clock the handbell is rung by Mrs. Duffield, the assistant teacher.

Hymn 47 is sung, each child concentrating hugely:

> *'Daisies are our silver,*
> *Buttercups our gold:*
> *This is all the treasure*
> *We can have and hold.'*

Then Sally Lewis reads a prayer she has composed: 'Dear God, we thank you for the daisies and the buttercups. We thank you for the rain and sun and wind and snow. We thank you for our lovely homes. Amen.' Garry Catchpole reads his prayer next: 'Dear God, thank you for all the animals like the birds. The country is a beautiful place and thank you for all the flowers. Amen.' Lucy shows us wood she has found with strange beetle marks, and Peter tells us how he made a floppy dinosaur which he stuffed with his mother's old stockings... so the day begins at Monks Eleigh Primary School.

Miss Cave has been teaching in East Anglia for 22 years, the last six as head of Monks Eleigh: 'I was in the telephone service once, for five years... but I had an aunt who kept telling me that I was wasting my own education just doing that. Father died when I was only six, you see, and my three sisters and I were brought up by our grandparents. I'm the only unmarried one — no, I'm not grumbling, you get tremendous fulfilment from teaching. Children give you a sense of being needed — that's something most of us must have. I was never very sure of myself, not really self-confident... when they asked me at my interview what I'd do if I felt I'd failed in a certain situation as a teacher I just said that I should blame myself, then have another go and make sure it worked next time. Well, I thought I'd made a mess of the whole thing, so I turned round and left the room. "Come back, Miss Cave," they called... they accepted me on the spot and I was sent to Wymondham in Norfolk for training.'

Joyce Cave is a comfortable person. She is comfortably built, comfortably dressed. She is a woman you take to instantly, feeling that she could not have an enemy on earth. She is sanity personified; it is inconceivable that her doctor has ever prescribed tranquillizers...

She is someone who, recognising her limitations, has accepted them amiably: 'People often want too much, I sometimes think. I suppose I've never set my sights too high. This is as far as I want to go . . . it's always been my ambition to be head of a little school and now I'm here no promotion in the world would ever make me leave. I waited 14 years until I could pluck up the courage to apply for a headship . . . so I've arrived, if you like.

'I share a nice house in Nayland . . . there's the Mercury Theatre in Colchester, walking the dogs, church every Sunday . . . I have a sense of carrying out what I've been guided to do. I think I'd be unhappy if I hurt anyone's feelings — perhaps I'm too appeasing. Selfless? (She is surprised, considering the idea for a moment.) No, I don't think of myself as selfless, but I suppose I don't really think about myself much at all. There's always been a strong sense of duty . . . heavens, does that make me sound pi?'

She laughs good naturedly — everything she does is good natured — and says it is time for morning break. She collects the handbell, following the children into the playing field where Rachel Nichols and Clive Newman are hanging upside down, like bats, from the exercise bars. A football trickles away from the players in her direction and she gives it a hefty, accurate boot towards the goal.

'They're outdoor children, they like being outside; but then they really seem to like everything. I hope I'm not being blind, but I seriously believe they're happy children. They come from stable homes, and parents back us to the hilt, they're so appreciative. They really do refute all the depression handed out by the media . . . broken marriages and misery, you'd think it was all like that. It's just the opposite here, about 100% stability — one broken marriage in the six years I've been here. The parents are farm workers, builders, from the gas company, someone from the East Anglia Tourist Board . . . I don't like to ask, it seems an intrusion. They're just very nice people and we all get on well together.

'I haven't had many problem children. There was one when I was teaching at Great Cornard School where there was a London overspill. He called me a really filthy name, so I put him in what I called the "nobody chair", where he'd just sit alone, not joining in with the others. He was only five and simply wanted a fight, and when he discovered he wasn't getting one he soon came round.

'No, we haven't any coloured children here. If we did, they'd stick out like sore thumbs at first, but only because they'd be different. The children would be intrigued... we had a little black girl at Cornard called Olu, but the children couldn't cope with the name, so they called her Lucy. But they noticed her as a new girl with a funny name, not a new *black* girl. We had another child with spina bifida — they accepted her totally, respecting all the things she tried to do.

'These Suffolk children... I keep coming back to the word "stable", well that's what they are. They're not over-articulate but they learn responsibility, and they all seem to have good aims, just expressed in different ways. They're not violent in any way, even when they play their Kojak games — and vandalism is unheard of. We rarely punish any of the children, and I have never believed in corporal punishment.'

Miss Cave and her 40 charges seem almost too good to be true. Clean children, they are; with lovely manners, well dressed and well fed, and always laughing. Yet what else should we expect of infants under nine years old? They are innocent when they arrive at Miss Cave's school and they are innocent when they leave; how else should it be? And at what stage and under what circumstances, one asks oneself, does this change? With a swimming pool and central heating and tasty school dinners cooked by Mrs. Harrison, it is a far cry from the day when Fred Buggs was beaten for stealing turnips. School milk froze in the bottle then, winter chilblains made little girls cry with pain, ink and chalk stained hands and clothes, and wet scarves steamed before coke stoves.

But the learning has not changed. There is still nothing abstract, nothing abstruse. 'Twice-three-is-six, three-sixes-are-eighteen. Our Father, which art in heaven. Our dinosaur is as long as ... God save the Queen.' Until school is over, then it is home to tea and immersion into an adult world which brings a child to maturity soon enough. Fred Buggs did not watch Kojak or Panorama; his horizons were the fields, the woods around Monks Eleigh. In the year of Fred's misdemeanour, Lenin died, a Republic was declared in Greece — but Fred knew none of these things. The village insulated him; giving him his essential needs and little else.

'I won't let what I see on television or read in the press bother me,' says Miss Cave. 'I'm very optimistic of the times we live in. I don't really know what would make me unhappy, even my retirement in seven years. By the time I'm 60 I shall have done a lot of work. Then I shall drive the old ladies near me to hospital. I didn't have a car until I was 35 and it's such a pleasure. Everything in my life is a pleasure.'

A recent pleasure was the school show they put on for parents. There was a Stone Age theme and Miss Cave dressed up in a wig, animal skin, and wore ear-rings of pine cones: 'One of the lines in the play had to be spoken by Clive – he had to say, "Be quiet, cave woman." The children loved that, my name being Cave.'

At the end of the show they all sang a song. You can hear it on tape, the children squealing with delight:

> *'Chocolate pud, chocolate pud,*
> *Whatever the problem, it does you good.'*

The Law: P.C. Ken Ives

IT IS UNLIKELY that the Mafia would be much interested in Wetheringsett-cum-Brockford. It is a place of hibernating quality, not given to violent waves of crime. True, of course, that the Americans stayed a while during the last war; but their acts of aggression were against Herr Hitler's Ruhr rather than the Suffolk Constabulary. When hostilities ceased, the aviators went home to Albuquerque, Martha's Vineyard, Sioux Falls, taking a couple or so local girls with them, while weeds took over their tarmac runway ... first weeds, then sugar beet, the land returning to its own.

Apart from that little episode, there have been few earth-shattering events since 1590 — except for Anglia Television erecting that damnable 1,000 ft. high mast: it is not a pretty sight, but then we must expect to make sacrifices for the exquisite gifts of *Opportunity Knocks* and *Coronation Street*.

What happened in 1590? The rector, Richard Hakluyt, an oceanographer of distinction, collected the narratives for his *Principal Navigations of the English Nation*. He worked in the rectory adjoining All Saints Church, with its fine 13th century arcade and its egregious Gothic organ standing at the east end of the south aisle.

By licence of his commission as Parliamentary Visitor of Suffolk Churches from the Earl of Manchester, William Dowsing did his best, or worst, to pillage All Saints. It seems to have been his vocation as well as his commission to destroy any church decoration that might be associated with papism, for he applied himself with consummate energy to his task. His work extended from 6th January 1643 to 1st October 1644, during which he visited 150 places in 50 days, leaving a diary account of his vandalism:

'No. 134 Wetheringsett. Aug the 26. 19 crosses. 16 about the Arches of the Church, and 3 on the Porch; a picture on the Porch a Triangle for the Trinity, to be done. Thomas Colby and Thomas Eley, churchwardens. Constables John Suton and John Genkthorne.'

The blessing is that sweet William, being pressed for time, moved hurriedly on from Wetheringsett to swing his pickaxe elsewhere, leaving All Saints relatively unmutilated. The first rector, Philip de Eye, appointed in 1229, might have turned in his grave at such goings on; yet he must have thanked his Maker that it could have been a deal more serious. Philip, a pious servant of the Lord no doubt, would have been much more affronted by the behaviour of a later incumbent to the living, a Mr. Ellis, 'rector' from 1883–1887.

Unfortunately, Mr. Ellis, curing the souls of Wetheringsett with apparent relish for four years, turned out not to have been ordained at all — a detail which came to light when his sister who kept house for him and with whom he had a row, split on him, thus costing the impostor seven years behind bars. Upon release, Mr. Ellis returned to visit the parish where he was, it is recorded, 'well received'. There remained, however, one or two questions in the minds of his forgiving flock. For example, Miss Kate Baker, who had been baptized by Mr. Ellis, was left wondering 'if it counted'. There was also the business of the marriages he solemnised...

The Parish Magazine of 1898 contains the following extract written by Mr. Ellis's successor, the Reverend C.F. Blyth:

'The Rector was lately asked by a woman who was (nominally) married to her husband by G.F.W. Ellis, at the time when he was passing as Rector of this parish, whether she is a lawful wife or not. It is important that it should be known that such marriages are not valid, but in this case an Act of Parliament dated Aug 13 1888, was specially passed to make them so. It is as follows: "Whereas George Frederick Wilfred Ellis forged certain letters of Orders, and falsely pretended himself to be in Holy Orders, and solemnised divers marriages according to the rights of the Church of England, and has been convicted of felony accordingly: and whereas doubts have been entertained as to the validity of the marriages so solemnised, and it is expedient to remove these doubts: Be it therefore enacted by the Queen's Most Excellent Majesty, by and with the advice and consent of the Lords Spritual and Temporal, and Commons, in this present Parliament assembled, and by the authority of the same, as follows: All marriages solemnised before the passing of this Act according to the rites of the Church of England by the said George Frederick Wilfred Ellis, between persons believing him to have been lawfully ordained, shall be as valid as if the same had been solemnised by a duly ordained clergyman of the Church of England." '

Whew! What a sigh of relief must have gone up from the beds of Wetheringsett village that sultry night of Aug 13 1888.

Born in another time, it might have been Police Constable Ken Ives' duty to arrest the erring priest; and hopefully Mr. Ellis would have come quietly because Ken Ives, a gentle man, has never used his truncheon in anger throughout 28 years' service. As we have seen, it is a peaceful beat covering 9,000 acres, including the adjoining parishes of Wickham Skeith, Thwaite, and Mendlesham, largely open agricultural country, flat, with few neurotic bumps, few schizoid declivities. Chicken stealing and poaching, these are about the depths of depravity hereabouts. Ken Ives knows everyone by name, by nick-name too; everyone knows him. He says, 'I haven't got a single villain on this patch.'

Until 1968 he covered the ground by foot and by cycle; then he became automated, driving a Ford Escort with the call-sign Juliet Two Bravo which he uses after each stop, reporting by radio to police headquarters at Martlesham. He looks back to his pre-combustible era nostalgically. He likes walking. He is used to it. Once, as a prisoner of war, he walked 600 miles as the Germans fell back before the Russian onslaught. 'On foot or bike you could stop. You saw a chap ditching and you'd stop: "Hullo, Charlie, how're the cabbages?" And he'd say, how are your roses, Mr. Ives. With a van, particularly in bad weather, you're inclined to stay in it — you lose a bit of contact. You used to be on your own. You were trusted. You saw the sergeant about once a week, and the Superintendent was a distant figure, not God exactly but... today you're under supervision all the time. Country coppers were characters in the old days.

'We had a terrible accident a few years ago up the road. The garage owner's wife was watering the flowers in her garden and this car's wheels locked and it went straight into the garden and killed her. I knew them. I mean, I used to have a cup of tea with them ... I organised the necessary things, how I did I don't know, and then I cried for the first time in my life. I had to deal with the body, you see, me and Johnny Self — he used to keep the streets clean — we both cried. The whole village was affected. It hit me more than anything in the war.'

Chicken stealing, poaching, traffic incidents; that is about the sum of Wetheringsett-cum-Brockford's skirmishes with the law. It is all in a day's work ... Ken Ives is over at Stoke Ash, directing the children's school crossing when an accident occurs, literally outside the police station — home also of Ken and his wife Gwen — on the Ipswich to Norwich road. An articulated lorry with a load of dog food, 32 tons laden, brakes suddenly to clear a left turning vehicle. The lorry jack-knifes, lurching across the road, blocking it so that an approaching giant charges into its armour. Broken glass and twisted metal, a shattered windscreen, steam; two monsters hissing impotently at each other on the A140 at 8.50 am precisely. One driver has a cut wrist, the other is shaken, both lucky to be alive. Dr. Beazer is on the way. Meanwhile, there is a bottleneck, a jam already a mile long in each direction. Ken Ives is taking details, a police Land Rover arrives, then another car. Tape measures, diversion signs, a constable sweeps away debris. No blood this time. By 9.25 am traffic is flowing again.

Gwen Ives makes coffee as Ken clears up. Then it is in the van, over to Wetheringsett, along Green Lane toward where Katy Garrod lives, one mile out of the village, in isolation. Nothing here but winter wheat and leafless trees; nothing except the promise of spring, a promise that snowdrops, aconites, and daffodil shoots are keeping. Katy loves her flowers. No time for people, but she loves the silent things, the growing, innocent things of nature. There is no threat in nature; only neutrality. There is no love either, not in neutrality. But Katy seems to do without the encumbrance of love, for she shrugged it off long ago when she turned her back on the village.

The chimney of her cottage has fallen in; there is a hole in the roof. Through the hole pours rain and sun with impartiality; and Katy worries not at all, moving from one room to another as matters get worse. It is the garden she is drawn to; stepping tenderly among the snowdrops, aconites, and the daffodil shoots, murmuring endearments to them.

So long is it since Katy had a conversation that it is difficult to understand her. She is very deaf too. Locked into silence and self-imposed exile, she has minted a language of her own, bright with images that a child might use. Not long ago she was ill: 'Thisey snakey-thing insidey me . . . Thinkey it gone awhy. All rightey now. Eh? Lonely? Not missey peoplies, no . . . nothing to missey isey? Talkie to peoplies dere . . . used to talkie to meself, now talkie to peoplies down derey.' She points to the stone floor. A cat pokes its head from a corner, then shoots out with a wail through the paneless window. Katy has two cats, both nameless.

In the centre of the room a saucepan of water boils on a paraffin burner. There is little furniture. The cottage has no electricity and no running water, so Katy draws water from a stream in the woods. She keeps warm by burning wood which she gathers from the hedgerows, loading it into her pram. Katy and her pram are familiar sights, but if she spots you, she will head off through the trees. Katy and her pram have been seen as far away as Eye, an eight mile walk each way.

If you knock on her door, she may answer and then again she may not. She does not invite company. She lives apart from cold and noise and pain. Perhaps she chooses not to be a witness to the hurt people do to each other. Her skin looks healthy, scrubbed and glowing. Her eyes are blue, unclouded. She had a beauty, not entirely faded. She eats tinned food, heated on her paraffin burner, but does not need much. No one has ever heard her complain or ask for more than she has. There is no radio in her cottage, no books, no family heirlooms; it seems unlikely that she hides banknotes under her mattress. Yet Ken Ives says a youth broke into Katy's cottage, to see what he could get away with.

Opposite All Saints Church is the post office. Winnie Smith is postmistress, as her father was postmaster before her, until a German bullet took away his life in the Great War. Sixty seven years the Smiths have been handling stamps, postal orders, pension books. The shelves carry huge apothecary jars, and there are notices for the Sadler's Wells Royal Ballet in Norwich, and a Colorado Beetle warning. They do not sell plastic toys and bubble-gum at Wetheringsett Post Office, its function being purist.

Winnie Smith is 68, quite young, she says; and two or three years older than Katy Garrod whom she remembers since childhood — Katy and her sister Marjorie, with brothers Walter, who died, and Gordon who lives in a caravan. 'She went into service, did Katy — Kathleen May we called her then — and she worked at Footmans in Ipswich once. She was a gorgeous needlewoman, and a painter, really clever with her fingers.

'Then she had a young man. I'd better not say his name . . . I used to see them walking, holding hands. She seemed ever so happy. I don't know what happened. She said she was going to have a baby, but she never did. Some people call her a recluse, others call her eccentric. She doesn't care for people too much. She comes in sometimes to collect her pension, but I don't think she spends much. Says she doesn't want a pension.

'She doesn't care for people, but people care for her. Marjorie shops for her, but she won't let anyone through her door — you were lucky. Flowers and nature is all she cares for. If I'm walking, I might see Katy a long way off. Do you know what she's doing? She's just standing there, gazing at trees and flowers.'

Juliet Two Bravo's next call is at the Manor; only today it is Wetheringsett Manor Hotel. A long, upward sweeping drive brings you to an 1843 baronial mansion, constructed from Woolpit brick, mellowing nicely, all set in 20 acres of parkland, including even a nine hole golf course. There is a cocktail bar with a rich claret coloured carpet you could sprain your ankle on, and a sophisticated menu including cornets of smoked salmon stuffed with prawns and rosemary sauce. They have some rare wines too, including a 1795 Madeira at £190 a bottle, an 1811 Napoleon Cognac for £170, and a 1945 Château Lafitte at £90.

But once a manor always a manor. 'Feudalism' is a word still featured in Wetheringsett's vocabulary; and locals do not feel comfortable about drinking beer beneath the spectral gaze of their dead squires. Well, that is the hotel manager's explanation.

'My wife and I had a wedding anniversary meal there once,' recalls Ken Ives, 'and I had a ploughman's lunch once, but it's usually the big farmers and businessmen who go. Locals drink at the White Horse.'

Which is a couple of miles away at Wetherup Street, the other side of Hockey Hill; and it has stood there, four-square and solid, a long time before 1843 if those stout beams are anything to go by. Miss Audrey Hammond has been licensee for 25 years, selling mints, gob-stoppers and liquorice as well as Whitbreads. Mr. Nunn and Mr. Chapman, both retired from looking after the County Council roads, are drinking, sharp on the dot of midday. The White Horse has a fruit machine today, and bingo sessions are held regularly. There is not much else to do, what with the nearest cinema all those miles away at Stowmarket; an impossible journey by bus.

'Good day, Mrs. Lacey,' says Police Constable Ives at the spot known as Lacey's Corner. 'Have you got that book for us to see?'

During the do-it-yourself alterations they found a book in a sealed up Dutch Oven. Its pages were covered with faded writing and child's drawings, like a diary. 'That book,' considers Mrs. Lacey. 'They said it should go to Ipswich, to the museum. Well, I don't know — I think we lent it to someone. My husband might know, but he's not come down today.'

We come across Albert Whatling next, a regular fund of stories, with a sharp enough memory for a man born in the last century. Scraping mud off his boots, he leads the way into his sitting room, busy with the ticking of clocks, glowing yellow with horse brasses. He likes telling of the day, how many years ago he cannot recall, when they accidentally knocked down a deer: 'Might have been from Helmingham. A dead deer aren't no good to no one, eh? So we skinned 'em. That did taste good.' When Mr. Whatling went to school he borrowed his brother's shoes, and if his brother needed them, no school that day. At 12 he was in the fields, earning his keep for 2s. 6d. a week. 'When I got old enough to vote, they told me, "You doan't vote conservative — that dew mean dear food." '

At Bridge House lunch is on the table, shoulder of mutton surgically carved by the senior partner of Wetheringsett's medical practice. Jean Lawton, a doctor herself, arrived in the village first, settling in until Edward's release from the Royal Army Medical Corps in 1945. They have been here ever since, listening to a stream, the Dove, flowing through their garden on its way to join the Waveney.

Edward treats the sick. Jean, no longer practising medicine, delves into village history, researching esoteric data: her notes tell you that in 1556 there was one marriage in Wetheringsett, two baptisms, four burials, in 1647 the harvest was disastrous. From 1620–1669 average yearly deaths amounted to 10.6, thus (since the death rate at the time was a fairly constant 32 per thousand) giving Wetheringsett a population of 328.6.

In 1740 Church accounts paid out 4d. for 1lb of nails for the steeple, and in 1896 Cassie Baker, clever child, obtained 287 marks out of a maximum of 288 at Sunday School. It is all there, neatly typed on exercise book paper.

Following in the footsteps of Philip de Eye, Richard Hakluyt, and the more wobbly ministry of Mr. Ellis, is the Reverend Paul Plumley, who came to this, a parish of 1,400 souls, after serving 14,000 in Mile Cross, Norwich, late in 1977. He is 35 years old, 'evangelical by persuasion', yet determined to take the 'middle stance'. He has four churches to look after but prefers to believe that the church is in 'people, not buildings'. He and his wife Pamela have great plans: restoration of the church fabric, less archaic forms of heating, they would like to open up more of the rectory, to see it used by London friends and by children. They have a long way to go, and this they know.

Back at the police station Gwen Ives describes her husband as a 'caring man'. Ask him about promotion, he replies that law books confuse him, that he isn't brainy enough for promotion: 'I enjoy coppering — that's what we call it. I'm good at that.'

It bothers him that Katy was burgled; he can't understand the mentality that would do such a thing: 'I mean, who'd want to harm her? Like Winnie Smith says, she loves nature. She talks to flowers. You can't steal from someone like that.'

The Verger: Alan Franklin

IT IS Lammas Day in Ely, 1st August — the day on which first-fruits were offered in Anglo-Saxon times. In truth there is a satiated feel about the place, an air of fecundity in the surrounding countryside: black fen soil is yielding. Men and women move slowly, the weight of summer upon their limbs. Flying insects are drowsy, listless, there may be a storm.

An orange and white coach with reclining seats and tinted windows pulls up outside the cathedral: *Hödl's Autoreisen*, reads the message along its gleaming shanks. German tourists alight. They wear long, pale raincoats, with matching faces; they form up symmetrically before their *führer* who directs their attention, heavenwards, to the towering West Front. 'Ja, ja,' they nod, aiming Leicas precisely as a firing squad.

An Italian group sprawls on Palace Green, an untidy, chattering litter, laughing and kissing, undisciplined and uninhibited. There are Japanese too, dark-suited and compact, bobbing and bowing at anything that moves. Australians there are, Americans, Africans . . . the world has come to Ely this Lammas Day.

A single figure, a man apart, enters the cathedral through the Galilee Porch. He is of average height, averagely portly for his 67 years; he knows where he is going, proceeding along the Nave, passing the Prior's Door on his right, passing Ovid's Cross. He passes five tablets let into the wall: they honour John Southby, who served the cathedral 60 years as verger; Henry White came next, with a reign of 58 years, then Joseph Fortesque, 25 years; Henry Hills, 46 years; and William Vaughan, 29 years. Between them 218 years' devotion to God and to His house. To say nothing of the past 37 years, when His servant Alan Franklin bore the mace — or verge — as badge-of-office of senior verger and sub-sacrist.

Mr. Franklin acknowledges his predecessors, continuing his progress towards the Octagon, an umbrella, unfurled, flapping, incongruous, hooked over one arm. Beneath the Lantern, built by Alan de Walsingham, he pauses to exchange the time of day with Canon George Youell who, finger tips together extended into the very shape of a church roof, has been asking children which corner of the globe they come from.

The verger explains that the stained glass above the Choir is Victorian, considered rather poor. But there is nothing poor in the quality of light filtering down: it is auroral, crespuscular. It is unearthly, being — should one believe in such fancies — God-sent.

And the verger . . . well, Mr. Franklin is no longer verger; he has handed over, retiring two years ago after a sherry party at which he was presented with an engraved silver salver, a cheque, and an address on parchment. His wife, always a 'good manager . . . she had to be on a verger's salary,' was handed a floral bouquet. Today they live in Deacon's Lane, in a flat of Thomas Parson's Charity, administered once by Cromwell before he became Lord Protector of England.

Alan Franklin's Norfolk-born mother went into domestic service to the Canon of Norwich Cathedral and Master of St Catherine's College, Cambridge, Canon Johns. His father had been a butler, but eventually went to sea as a steward, transferring — fatefully — from the Australia run to the *Titanic*. When the liner went down, he was pulled from the water but died of exposure, to be buried at Halifax, Newfoundland. Alan's mother did not remarry, bringing up her son and a daughter in her own way: 'She was desperately hard-working, strict and straight-laced. One drink was bad, two unthinkable — but the old dear liked her glass of port at Christmas.

'Hard work never killed anyone, was her motto; but when I wanted to be a chorister at Norwich Cathedral, she said, "I can't afford it." Luckily, she didn't have to . . . we had a visitor at school one day, a Dr. Bates, who asked me if I'd like to be one of his choir boys. I couldn't rightly understand that — at the tender age of seven I thought a "doctor" was a Doctor of Medicine. I'd never heard of doctors of music. Anyway, I was shortlisted from lots of boys and became a chorister . . . music and singing always meant a great deal to me.

'I remember — in 1926 it was — Queen Mary was

attending a service in the cathedral and she asked to meet the boy singing the solo. Well, that was me ... she was a very regal person, tall and very sweet, and she took me by the hand. I remember running all the way home to Sunday lunch and telling mother I'd never wash my hands again.'

Yet music was not to be Alan Franklin's immediate calling: 'I had a yen to go to sea, so I signed on as steward on the White Star Line. Odd thing was my first ship was the *Megantic*, and the first trip in her was to Halifax. So I found out where they'd buried the *Titanic* dead and went to see my father's grave — I wasn't one year old when he died, you see. I took this photograph of the grave.' He pulls out a faded, sepia print from his wallet; it is battered, but you can still see the headstones, stark as skulls.

'I stayed afloat until what we called the Sea Depression when I got a job as footman-valet to Lord Somerleyton near Lowestoft. But I soon went back to sea, on the *Jarvis Bay* to Australia. Lord Somerleyton was annoyed about that, he didn't want to lose me. Then, when I was 22, I married a shorthand typist from the Norwich Town Clerk's office ... she laughs at that now because they're all called "secretaries" today.

'After a bit my wife prevailed on me to give up the sea, so I started training as a sales representative selling carbon paper, but somehow it wasn't me. So I chucked that and went to the British Home Stores in Ipswich when it opened ... only there wasn't much chance of promotion, so we parted company.

'Then in 1939 I saw an advertisement in the *Church Times* saying Ely Cathedral needed a verger by Michaelmas ... and I just knew it would be my life. I saw Dean Cranage, who knew me, and he gave me a letter of reference ... 90 applicants there were and I got the job, nearly 40 years ago that was.'

We are sitting on a wooden bench in the Cathedral Parlour: 'It used to be the coal and coke store, so we called it the Chapel of St. Anthracite,' quips the verger. (It is difficult not to call him the verger; he has relinquished the post, but not the presence ... deprived of mace and cassock, he seems slightly naked, but still verger.) 'Chapel of St. Anthracite': it is one of his little jokes. He is fond of his little jokes, finding them mildly shocking, impious. Ask him if he would have liked to take the cloth, he replies:

'No, *never* . . . I'm far too worldly.' His little jokes reveal his worldliness; he laughs at them himself, quietly enjoying the wickedness of his innocence.

'From 1941 to 1946 I was in the Royal Navy,' he recalls, 'on South Atlantic convoys in corvettes, H.M.S. *Burdock* and H.M.S. *Crocus*. They sent me up to the Admiralty for a commission, but I failed — still I did better financially, coming out as a Chief Petty Officer. Talking about religion, I used to serve at the altar at Chatham Naval Barracks and everyone asked, "Do you have religious mania?" And I said no, I was just a believer, a worldly person. I see God as one who maps out our lives, he overrules us and our lives. Death? That *is* the problem, we none of us know, we have to believe — no one's come back to tell us. I'd always rather help than hamper, but people aren't always receptive to kindness. The thing about being a churchman is that you try to do unto others as you would have them do unto you.'

The St. Anthracite benches are hard, so we stretch our legs along the massive Nave, among the Germans and the Japanese being Bo-peeped by their guides. The Germans are giving their thorough attention to a sign: *Wilkommen — eintritt ist frei aber eine spende von 20p. pro besucher trägt dazu bei, den dom zu erhalten*. It is in Japanese too, this appeal for 20p; in eight languages in all . . . only another £270,000 needed to restore the tower. There are T-shirts and micro-pants, rucksacks and tracksuits. The verger makes a face: 'I hate to see these changes today . . . ice-cream, people throwing toffee wrappers about, men wearing hats . . . smoking. I tell them — I've got a sensitive nose. *Television crews . . . !*' (He makes the latter sound like the Four Horsemen of the Apocalypse.) 'I like dignity and discipline — you got six of the best in the old days. Some people just don't treat the place for what it is.'

Through the screen, in the exquisitely carved 14th century choir-stalls, a choir practises: 'Murrill in E. My Soul, there is a country — Parry.' The choristers are in scarlet cassocks, white ruffles at the throat. Organ sounds swell, like a rising sea; you could drown in such music. 'Anyone playing that thing for the first time has to be careful,' warns the verger. 'You could blot out the whole choir. I know a bit about it . . . in 1947 Dr. Sydney Campbell, the organist, invited me to join the cathedral choir and there I stayed for 26 years. I love oratorio — my wife thinks I have that kind of belief for sacred music.

'I've enjoyed concerts in the cathedral, but it's taken me a long time to acclimatize to applause. Sir Adrian Bolt, a lovely man, wouldn't have it — said he was making an offering to God. Yes, applause used to make me feel a bit sick actually . . . but the masses won. Old Barbirolli liked applause . . . Richter's recital was memorable, so was the Verdi Requiem, and Yehudi Menuhin . . . what a charming man he is. These great people are so humble — I suppose humility makes greatness.'

For 37 years the verger has trod these stones, preceding the Dean in ceremony, bearing his mace as today he bears his umbrella . . . and how he knows his cathedral, every nook and cranny. He directs your attention above the choir-stall canopies on the south side, at the joining of the first two arches above the choir, to a grotesque in stone known as the 'Ely Imp'. It seems that there are two heads, one above the other; but the verger points out that they are in fact pick-a-back. He knows also the doggerel which has been handed down, the origin of which is too obscure even for him:

> 'Ely Imps you see,
> 'Pick-a-back imps in glee
> With the wings of a bat!
> And the grin of a cat,
> Mocking at you and me,
> Sing nonny ho, nonny he,
> Oh what fools poor mortals be!

In 1349 Walsingham completed work on the Lady Chapel, dedicated to Our Lady, the Virgin Mary. It is a building of immense, blinding purity, light cascading from the tracery of plain glass windows. At the time of the Reformation in 1539 much of the carving was mutilated, yet it would take considerably more vandalism to impair the perfection of the Lady Chapel. The verger is speechless. The Japanese are speechless, smiling polite, toothy smiles at the single span roof.

'You should hear the singing in here,' whispers the verger. 'Such acoustics — listen to the echo . . .' With which he throws out his chest, emitting a forceful round

'G'. The note reverberates, an artillery barrage of sound in the stillness. The Japanese are startled, the Germans unmoved — the Italians full of wonder, comfortable in excesses.

Still so much to see, so many glories in this palace of prayer founded by Queen Etheldreda in the year 673 A.D. The verger is in his stride, in his heaven you could say; and yet he has saved the best till last, the choicest, most esoteric of memorabilia. He leads the way along passages, unlocks a door and then another; until we are standing in what to all the world looks like a lumber room. Something, just a shape, is shrouded in brown paper. With a flourish in which pride and humility grow as one, the verger unveils a bust — the head and shoulders of a chunky, slightly pugnacious fellow wearing spectacles, thumbs hitched behind lapels in the way of an orator. It is the verger, immortalised in stone.

Outside the Lady Chapel scaffolding is up. Eventually, and it may take a long while yet, three likenesses will be arranged in place, as gargoyles were in olden days. One of them will be the verger, a fixture and fitting for perpetuity, vigilant as ever, for ever.

The verger looks up, his eyes beyond the scaffolding. A wind stirs, clawing at his umbrella; the storm is coming. He seems to be searching his mind, looking perhaps for one of his little jokes — which eludes him.

He says, perhaps too fiercely for the occasion: 'Undoubtedly, I've felt a lot of love from this place.'

The Lifeboat Coxswain: Richard Davies

TWO SOLITARY figures, wrapped in oil-skins against the slanting rain, are fishing from Cromer pier. It is like an iron dinosaur, this pier, stranded on a sandbar; there is a primeval look about it which has little to do with a supersonic age. As you pass through the stuttering turnstile, the Amusement Arcade is dead ahead; next comes the Pavilion: 'Nightly at 8.15 Spectacular Top Quality Family Show.' At the end of the pier is the lifeboat slipway.

Dominating the scene is the Hotel de Paris, fanciful, baroque, its turrets and hodge-podge of pedimented dormers belonging somehow to a Victorian pantomime. George Skipper, the designer, liked his bit of fun; no doubt he sat at his drawing board tongue in cheek. And why Hotel de Paris? The best we can do is trace, to an 1834 directory, a certain Mr. Pierre le Francois who is listed as manager of a boarding house he christened the Hotel de Paris.

Behind the Paris is a maze of back streets, each one narrow as a puritan's smile. On the wall of Swallow Cottage in Corner Street is a plaque commemorating Cromer's seafaring hero, Henry Blogg. Across the way, at number 9, lives Richard Davies, coxswain of the R.N.L.I. lifeboat.

You go upstairs to the sitting room, where there are portraits of six generations of Davies, each one coxswain of Cromer's lifeboat. There is a photogravure of the old *Louise Heartwell* lifeboat putting to sea; a table lamp is in the shape of an anchor; and there are three aquaria, bubbling quietly away, full of tropical fish. On the floor is a half-finished crab-pot Richard Davies is making, his 'homework', as he calls it.

'The lifeboat's not a job. The crew are all volunteers except the mechanic, that's Ralph, he's full time. My real job's inshore fishing, crabs and lobsters, that's our bread and butter. Julie, the wife, runs the shop — we sell wet fish and shell-fish — and we sell to other shops. I've got a beach boat, Norfolk crabbers we call them, open deck,

22 feet 6 inches long, with a 50 h.p. Thorneycroft — she cost £6,000. I've got a crew of one, Clive Rayment. It's a seven day week unless there's a wind blowing. We listen to the shipping forecast, then we're away by daybreak, out to about four miles and back again five or six hours later.

'We have 170 pots out and a good haul's about 1,500 crabs, but there's no such thing as average — you never can tell. You might get 1,500 in March and only 90 in July. Spring, that's our harvest time. Then we have to sell them — used to get them up to London, but the train's so bloody expensive now. No, the sea's not running out of crabs, but you might get seven good years followed by seven lean years, that's the way it goes. We get poor hauls when there's cod about . . . when crabs moult, their shells are soft and the cod eat them.'

Richard Davies is 33 years old and was educated 'very slowly' at the local Secondary Modern. 'I was below average intelligence,' he tells you. He has red hair and a fierce red beard; there is a tattoo on his right forearm. He looks tough, competent, piratical. His fingers are spatulate, yet deft as he works with the net for his crab-pot. He wears a heavy fishing jersey; he seldom wears anything else. Julie says he even insisted on taking it to Majorca on holiday when the temperature was in the 80's. 'No, I didn't,' he corrects her. 'I took three.' He is guarded at first, eyeing you speculatively, assessing whether you are trying to make a fool of him. It wouldn't do to make a fool of Richard Davies; those spatulate fingers would make a beefy fist. He is probably quick-tempered, mercurial.

'I hated the sea when I was a kid, detested it. I wanted to work on a farm with animals, but I didn't have any choice — had to do what the old man said — so I went to sea when I was 15, straight from school. I loathed it. I was seasick every day for two years . . . then, after a year, I began to like it, despite being sick — being sick is a habit, like coughing or spitting. Now I wouldn't change it for the world, I love it — you're boss, your own boss, I couldn't work in a factory. There's freedom and competition at sea, 14 other crabbers all working the same stretch of sea, all trying to earn a living.

'The lifeboat? Well, that's a family tradition, a Cromer tradition too . . . there was even a lifeboat on the school badge, and when we heard the maroon — the lifeboat gun — we'd all go into the school assembly to say prayers for the lifeboat crew. You were proud of them. In a crew of seven there was my father, grandfather, one uncle and a cousin.

'I had my first trip when I was 16 — you're meant to be 17. so they only took me out on fine days. I was made coxswain two years ago and now I'm always on call — used to like a drink but not any more, just in case. If I leave the town my cousin Billy, he's second coxswain, he has to be on call.

'What happens is this: a ship in distress gives the Mayday signal to the coastguards, and also her position. The coastguards inform the local R.N.L.I. secretary who rings me, and I fire two maroons at the back of the house — and everyone starts running like hell. From pub or bed or wherever, we launch the lifeboat three minutes after the maroons, *three minutes*. She's a 37 ft. Oakley with two engines sound as a double decker bus. She's a self-righter ... oh, she could capsize but she'd come back up again.'

He laughs. It is a raw, hoarse sound, showing white, even teeth. He is relaxing. Suddenly, as if to show his trust, his way of letting you know you have passed the test, he offers drinks: whisky, gin, beer he has. He passes the cigarettes: 'They're only Woodbines,' he apologises. Julie makes him another cup of coffee, then curls up on the floor, munching an apple. She has taken off her shoes, the gesture endorsing her husband's acceptance of a stranger.

'This is the slowest year. We're usually called out about every three weeks, but it's been months since the last time, no launching since Christmas Eve. I don't know how many times we've launched since I became coxswain — you don't count, that's not the point, you just try to do a good job. Each time it's memorable — there's always something. Sometimes being wrecked puts people off the sea — you can never tell if a man will go back, but it takes a hell of a lot to put a man off the sea. Somehow you just remember the good times.

'Frightened?' (He considers the question gravely, as if it is a new idea.) 'Well, I don't know ... when there's a gale or a sandbank ... I don't know if it's fear or respect, but you always know that the sea's the governor. No one's been lost from the lifeboat for years. Last crewman to be lost was in wartime action when six from a crew of 12 went overboard and only five came back: all but one was a relative of mine — if they'd gone, the family would have been wiped out. Yes, there are a lot of sandbanks well out to sea here, they shift a little and build up. You must know where you are, but we have radar now — used to be a compass, the watch and a log, that's all. A lot of wind here too — wind and tide, and the two together mean trouble.'

There was trouble the night of 16th November 1977 for the 546 ton coaster *Nimrod* which had left Whitstable bound for Leith with a cargo of 476 tons of gravestone chippings. The *Nimrod's* 161 feet plunged off on a course towards the Dudgeon Light Vessel. By the early morning the wind had increased from the south-west to gale force nine, gusting 10. By now the *Nimrod* was 20 miles north of Cromer, rolling heavily from a violent beam sea. The gravestone chippings — an ironic cargo — had slipped to starboard, and every time she rolled she increased her angle to starboard.

At 03.47 *Nimrod* sent out a Mayday signal and the Cromer lifeboat was launched. Meanwhile, six ships in the vicinity had altered course and were heading towards the stricken vessel; but at 05.45 she went down, her crew jumping from her stern minutes earlier. Coxswain Davies and his men picked up the *Nimrod's* crew, but not until they had been in the winter sea for an hour and a half.

'What did we think about? No time for thinking about anything other than the job and how to tackle it — wondering whether, at 10 knots, you'll get there in time and, if you do, whether you'll spot them. A man can't last long in that kind of sea. You get their clothes off first and get them into warm blankets — no, you don't feed them rum or brandy, that shocks the system. You never get two men the same — mostly they're numb, grateful, but usually silent.

'Oh, don't worry, I know there's a God. The sea's made me pray — fright, I suppose. I don't pray much ashore, but out there if fear's on your mind God helps, doesn't he? Yes, 'course I want my son, John, to go to sea — he's 13 but even keener than me.'

Julie: 'No, I wouldn't stand in John's way. I can't see him or Richard working in suits in an office job. I worry — I can't switch off until the lifeboat's back, but I follow on the V.H.F. I listen to what's going on on board. It keeps me in touch, and I can't sleep . . . it's a long wait.'

Richard: 'You get very close to each other out there; like it's one man thinking instead of eight. You almost know what a man will do . . . there's no second chance . . . it rules our lives.'

Julie: 'I can't see him ever finishing with the sea — he couldn't live inland. He suffers from landsickness. He's always going out, just to look at the sea.'

Richard: 'I'll hate handing over to John — I'll never let go. I'll be the same as my father, if I live that long . . . when we go out fishing in the morning Dad's standing on the cliffs watching us. When we come back, hours later, he's still there . . . I don't think he's moved.'

The G.P.: Dr. Sarah Hampton

'IF YOU REALLY want to know why I became a doctor, it's because I can't resist looking into other people's houses. No, I'm being quite serious; I have this *thing*, this fascination for seeing the way people live — what they spend money on, their furniture, what they eat, how they behave in their own homes. I'm a professional Nosey Parker.

'It's not totally that, of course. I mean, I could have become a char or an *au pair* to cross that threshold. It was largely rebellion as well . . . rebellion against the artistic side of my family. My mother and father both paint . . . you wouldn't think a bus driver would paint in his spare time, would you? Oh yes, I'm very working class, but my parents had this love for music and painting. I wanted to better myself. I wanted a career, not just a job.

'I had a long time to think about it. I had congenital spondylolisthesis at 14, a congenital abnormality . . . a bent back and a scar down one leg where they removed some bone. For six months I was flat on my back in hospital; it gave me a chance to look at hospital life — and I liked what I saw. It also gave me the chance to study, to cut off from everything else — it was all hell apart from 'A' levels and medicine. So this is what I clung to.'

Sarah Hampton is 27 and looks older. She is a tall, gangling woman, making sudden darting movements of mind and body; movements which are almost phrenetic, time-defying. She glances, covertly, at her watch as she talks, subtracting minutes from her day. She decides that there is time for coffee, so crosses the Common Room of the Medical Centre where she works to plug in the kettle. Each act is economical, designed to a specific purpose: whether adding milk to Nescafé, scanning a case history, or recalling her own past, the attention to detail, the concentration is formidable. One senses that her breakfast four minute eggs would not be cooked in three minutes 50 seconds.

All the same, there is a complexity about her. Seeming so secure, she somehow reveals her insecurity. The bonhomie with which she greets staff and patients emphasises her shyness. Her total abandonment of subterfuge exposes her self-consciousness. She seems an immensely intricate person, a woman struggling.

'I managed to get a university grant to read medicine. It was dreadfully lonely at first because I had no social graces. I'd never been out to dinner, never drunk wine . . . you've no idea what a stigma it can be to have parents without a car or telephone when you begin to mix with a posher set. Yes, I was made to feel ashamed of them. Not now, now I'm proud of them; the system made me ashamed of them. Rather sad, they think I'm above them today.

'You see, I looked on myself as a cripple — you know, a hunchback no one could love. I thought no man would ever want to go to bed with me, let alone marry me. So I worked instead. I knew that if I became a doctor I'd be a person in my own right. Then I made friends with a bio-chemist whose father was a dustman, and things got better.

'I started going out with men, two or three boyfriends I had each term. I was a bit of a flirt, realising men didn't regard me as a freak. I found I had a rapport with them. My husband and I met at university . . . it was rather cynical of me: he's a brilliant academic, he had a car, he was good to be seen with . . . and he was interested in me. We married when I qualified at 24. He's an historian. We shan't have children. Why? They'd stop us doing so many things we want to — so it's for purely selfish reasons. Yes, I'm honest. Why be anything else?'

Erpingham Medical Centre is a red-brick building at the centre of a town with one foot in East Anglian industry, the other in agriculture. The practice has a team of five doctors serving 14,000 patients, the majority of whom are town-dwellers living in mean terraced council houses on nondescript estates. At 8.45 a.m. Sarah Hampton is completing her paper-work, checking emergency calls which have come in by telephone. She signs a letter recommending a 16 year old for an abortion: 'She wouldn't admit to intercourse at first . . . she was just hurt and confused. The boyfriend had chucked her to marry another girl, her parents wanted her to abort . . . she, poor girl, wants the child, but she's been talked out of it. Reasoned out of motherhood.'

At 9 a.m. Sarah sets off in her mini. Today all her calls are in the town and nearby village housing estates. It is the latter she is most bitter about: 'It's the lonely-bored belt. There are no amenities, no shops, no village spirit. It's no-man's land for rising, white collar lower management, leaving their wives alone all day . . . what else? So at weekends they need to pep things up a bit, with wife-swapping parties. No, you don't believe it, do you? Not of gentle, backward-looking, virtuous old East Anglia — but I get the wives in surgery telling me they're pregnant by other women's husbands. No, it is *not* all that uncommon.'

The first call is to see Mary, a 60 year old asthmatic: 'She's a nice old duck and basically her condition is psychosomatic. Her brother is dying of cancer and they are so close that she relates to his illness, sharing his pain. But she still needs medication, she needs attention and the reassurance of a doctor's visit.' After leaving the house: 'Poor old thing's in a terrible state today. She's had an electricity bill for £70 . . . she got £20 of it from the social services, but she's worried sick about the other £50. She can't really grasp that keeping warm costs so much.'

The next visit is to a small detached house on a well-tended estate. Two cars are in the driveway. Jane and her husband, both schoolteachers, have decided to start a family and Jane has just returned home from hospital after her confinement: 'I've never seen a happier mother. They're both thrilled, and it's a perfect baby. The mother said hospital was like a first class hotel, but she didn't like the consultant because he "patronised" her, so she'll have the next one at home. I *knew* their house would be as it is — beautifully done, close-fitted carpets, hi-fi, every modern gadget — it all fits somehow. I was dreadfully wrong once . . . this very scruffy man, *dirty* actually, used to come to surgery and I thought I bet this house is mucky; but when I was called there it turned out to be immaculate. He was a pigman, you see, and the only time he could get to surgery was straight from work.'

Next on the list is Fred: 'He came in nine months ago complaining that he'd been coughing up rusty coloured sputum and that he'd got a lump on his neck. Carcinoma of the lung was suspected and they opened him up — but it was inoperable. He's *riddled* with cancer, but he simply won't die. Oh, he knows all right and he wants to go, he's had enough, he knows how it affects his wife ... she's being a wonderful nurse. He's on 25 milligrams of Diamorphine and 10 milligrams of cocaine, mixed together and flavoured with peppermint, every hour. The usual dose is five to 10 milligrams of Diamorphine every six hours. I'm killing him with drugs, but he gets up, still smokes his cigarettes ... he just said to me "I shan't be here when you come on Friday, doctor ... "; but he should have been dead weeks ago. He watches that lump grow day by day, he chokes on his own sputum — and still he smokes. Makes you think ... the human body is a very tough piece of machinery.'

'Old Bessie' comes then: 'Dear old lady, she's over 90. "Doctor," she says, "me bowels won't work, I'm that bunged up." It's just old age and the plumbing getting faulty, that's all.'

Outside number 18 Sycamore Drive we coincide with the district nurse in her yellow Renault: 'Mrs. Chase is the colour of your car today,' Dr. Hampton tells the nurse. 'She's another who should have died a couple of months ago. When we told her she had carcinoma of the caecum, she put her hand on her Bible and said, "I'm ready anytime, doctor, the Lord will take me." But she's still at number 18, the colour of that Renault, with the neighbours reading the Bible to her. "Oh, I feel so much better today, doctor," she says. She's oozing gratitude ... she's dying well, that one.'

The morning passes. This is the way it goes until 11.15 a.m. when Sarah returns to the Centre for a two hours' surgery. Shortly after 1 p.m. she takes sandwiches to the Common Room where the partners have a working-lunch to discuss practice problems. More visits from two until 4.30 p.m., when there is another surgery; normally she gets away at 6.30, home to cook supper. Often she is delayed far later.

'Well, it can't be helped. There's a deep commitment to being a doctor. My husband can't come first; certainly not my social life. My patients come first, full stop. That doesn't mean to say I don't try to escape ... when we go out, I like to be "Mrs.", not "Doctor". Soon as people hear you're a doctor, their attitudes change: they either put on this huge act as if they hadn't even heard you were a doctor or they wheedle in bits about their symptoms, trying to manoeuvre opinions from you. Medicine can submerge you — that's why we must have other interests. You can't afford to be emotionally involved. I'm pretty good at switching off, but when I do become involved . . . oh boy! It cost me a lot of sleep once. I was delivering a baby when the one in 50,000 happened . . . the mother suffered a massive brain haemorrhage in delivery. When she died it hit me horribly — I couldn't understand.

'I can't understand East Anglians really . . . they're strange beasts, you never know what to expect. They have a language all their own. If a wife says of her husband, "He's a bit queer, doctor," it could mean he had anything from mild eye-strain to a near-fatal coronary. If she says, "He's whoolly queer, doctor," then you know you've got trouble . . . if he's not in his coffin by then. Then there's this word "rove" — they keep using it and I've never heard it anywhere else. It means a scab — now where did the word come from? They're forthright too. No messing around. The usual form at the surgery is, I say, "How can I help you?" and they reply directly, "It's me bladder . . . it's me corns". No euphemism.

'Another thing, did you notice today? I knock at the front door and they always answer from the back door. Then they take me through the kitchen into the best room, the parlour, which is next to the front door. In other parts of the country they'd be ashamed to take the doctor in through the back door. It's something I notice all the time.

'But they're easy to get on with, you know where you stand. It's those who've come to settle or retire here who can be trying. Sounds far-fetched, I know, but sometimes they don't know what to expect. The winter east wind shocks them, the gales scare them . . . but the main differences aren't between East Anglians and non-East Anglians, but between townees and country folk. In the country they tolerate more pain before asking for help, they apply self-medication . . . grandma's old recipe of glycerine and honey, and jolly good it is. I approve of that. The townee cries out for help at the slightest twinge, they want prescriptions, instant-miracle cures. It's largely a case of a little knowledge . . . magazine articles, T.V. programmes ... they help breed phobias. People recognise names today: so tiredness becomes leukemia, headaches become brain tumours. We're more hypochondriacal. If the newspapers cover, say a concern for women smokers over 35 who are on the pill, we get a rash of 35 year old women to surgery.

'That's one aspect of the cause and effect of various standards today. There's a good side: the best preventative medicine is better housing, better diet ... and then again, too much better diet encourages obesity, cars encourage the sedentary life. It seems that you can't win — except we *are* winning if you wish to applaud the fact that we live longer.'

This is off-duty talk, away from the Medical Centre, the telephone. She is not on call, and yet there is a tenseness about her. She sips a glass of sherry, making it last an hour or so. Her husband listens attentively, offering no contribution: the floor is hers. Only when the conversation becomes non-medical, neutral, does her separateness dissolve. He is used to this, referring to the condition as his 'husband-of' syndrome, the 'subordinate role'. Then they talk of Rome, of the progress of the Great Plague, of country footpaths; and they share, coming together. Sarah's separateness is a fact of her concentration, the convictions to which she returns.

'It's less the quantity of life, if you like, than the quality that concerns me. So we've got rid of chronic bronchitis caused by damp housing; and what do we have instead? Diseases of stress: job anxiety, mortgage-itis, school fee-fever, loneliness. Women suffer more because they are not so stretched in other fields, they are turned in upon themselves more.

'It's so much easier to treat organic sickness. You know that "Farmers' Lung" is caused by mouldy hay fungus; you anticipate bad backs when the harvest is at its height, with men bouncing along in combines; you know kids contract diarrhoea and vomiting during crop spraying ... you diagnose and prescribe. What do you prescribe when a man's passed over for promotion, when a wife feels neglected?'

She looks distressed and, conscious of the transparency of the distress, laughs deprecatingly: 'Oh, well — we're all survivors. Few of us are in medicine for the vocation; I really believe that. Yes, it is a melancholy statement. It's all so convoluted: the National Health Service, private schemes . . . no, I'm not opposed to private medicine. If my father needed a hernia operation and could afford to pay, it would be done next week . . . there's an 18 months' wait for a National Health patient in Ipswich. Society *is* unequal and I see no alternative to this. The rich have, and the poor have not. I can't help enjoying my personal position in this society.

'I'd still become a doctor, given the choice again; and I'd be a G.P. You're part of the community, part of the family . . . you see the whole family, you're not in isolation as in hospital work. I'm interested in the whole person, not the diagnosis in isolation.

'I suppose I came into medicine more to cure myself than to cure others, but I like to think I'm learning. There's something very noble . . . well, let's just say that I'm learning more consideration and understanding of other dimensions.

'Would it help me accept the situation if terminal cancer was diagnosed in me? I refuse to comment on that. How the hell can I tell? How can anyone tell until it happens? Does anyone want, really *want* to die? Especially of cancer? I've seen it . . . and it's not pretty.'

The Stranger: Thomas McIntosh

TOM MCINTOSH is a 39 year old American from Washington, D.C., whose home is the Old School at Hadleigh in Suffolk. He is a concert pianist who, at the age of 12, performed a Mozart Concerto with the National Symphony Orchestra of Washington. When he made his New York debut four years later, the *New York Times* commented: 'impressive, we look forward to his next appearance.' In recent years he has been appointed conductor of the City of London Chamber Orchestra. As a pianist and conductor, his concert tours in both hemispheres have taken him to over 50 countries.

Immaculate credentials indeed for a peripatetic musician; but the single credential marking him as a man of common sense as well as talent was his decision in 1971 to make his home in East Anglia. The Old School in Hadleigh is both his house and concert hall; it is Victorian, adapting cheerfully to the tropical temperatures of American-adjusted central heating. The house is the venue for events organised by the Brett Valley Society for the Arts.

'I'd always lived in big cities — Washington, New York — so I had no idea what small town life was about. My move to Britain was a gradual process, nothing dramatic — I wasn't in rebellion. I wanted to live abroad for a while, to see my own society in a different light. Why East Anglia? Friends — musical friends who, during that era of inexpensive property of the 60's, had become involved in the cottage-industry, that of buying and doing up. I stayed 10 weeks with them and loved it. It was strange to me, utterly different yet not at all alien — I suppose my humble background comes from farming stock. I suppose it sounds corny to say it was like coming home; there was a rapport I'd never had living in big cities.

'Certainly in that summer I experienced none of the wariness or hostility towards strangers which is often quoted as being evident in the East Anglian character; but you see I was a *total* stranger, a tourist, and as such received a great deal of courtesy. So far as my relationships with them now, I do find people initially shy and reserved. The outsider has to make the first approach; and it's got to be done in a manner that's not frightening to them.

'However, when a stranger comes to live among them, particularly in a small town, there is the establishment of a pecking order, and one either loses or wins this little battle — this is where I felt downright discourtesy when I moved in from a number of people, four or five. Part of it has been ironed out, and I'm not at all sure it wouldn't have happened in the United States. I think the rather "exotic" work I'm in, and my own cosmopolitan background are not really conducive to small town living ... some people were afraid of me before I moved in. It's all to do with accents, what you do — I'm a bachelor living alone, no wife to make those first contacts in the street, in the shops ... perhaps it was a little more difficult for me.

'Every society has its pecking order — the terms of respectability in a town; who does what. There are those you'd dislike, but if you feel hard done by you couldn't bring it out in public because everyone would take sides with the establishment — not because that establishment is liked so much, but because it is *there,* representing respectable virtues.

'Yes, I've made friends. I set out to make friends. One thing that helped me enormously was having an art society, it's brought me into contact with a wide spectrum of the community who might not come if I invited them to my home, but who will come to the society's events — so their fear of my strangeness is overcome.'

After several years, Tom McIntosh is becoming part of the local scenery, recognised, nodded to, accepted. Accepted, perhaps, in the manner of a family conscious of good manners, yet reserving ultimate loyalties for blood relatives. 'I'm known now — and liked, I think. At least, I find it difficult to do errands locally because you have to spend 20 minutes talking to everyone you meet. They know me as Tom McIntosh and they address me as Tom. And I call them by their first names. They know exactly what I'm doing because everyone knows what everyone else does in Hadleigh. Not so much scandalizing in the sense of FitzGerald calling his boat *Scandal* after

Woodbridge's chief occupation . . . not so much that as an eagerness to know about another human being, but not in a malicious way. There's an enormous curiosity, and a little bit of fear of the unknown.

'The English love an eccentric more than we Americans do, but I'm not sure that your down-to-earth East Anglian farmer tolerates him. I mean, one very old local said to me recently: "Everything's fine about you, Tom, except that you're a pianist." This was the one unsettling quality to him. With old established families living in grander houses . . . perhaps I'm seen to have stolen some of their thunder by starting something for the community here. I've extended a hand they might not have wanted to take. But I think I'm welcome in most of their homes. There is always a little clique who bar certain interlopers without the acceptable pedigree. But I'm very touched by the basic warmth of most neighbours here; I feel totally secure in calling on anybody for help. Yes, Hadleigh cares . . . it may exact a retribution once an emergency is over, but I know I could walk into any house in Hadleigh for help and it would be given. As for the humour – well, after a few years I find it a rather self-deprecating one, turned back on themselves; rather in the sense of Jewish humour.'

One of the East Anglian's legendary characteristics is that he is supposed to be slow to change, resisting innovation as he would bubonic plague. 'I can't deny that it's uphill work. There's no denying a kind of apathy . . . that may be too strong a word – laziness, or sheer comfortableness with their own order of things. There is a reservation about the new which has to be overcome. I've tried to explain that the arts aren't snobbish, but a natural and necessary part of their lives . . . there's still an inclination not to part with money unless it's absolutely unavoidable! I can get very irritated with the East Anglian; dislike, no, because you actually see them wanting to do something if they could just break down this barrier of habit, self-consciousness. The arts are still equated with snobbishness and weirdness, and people here are conscious of Mrs. Next-Door's opinion.'

Of the scenic and architectural impact the countryside of his adoption has upon him, Tom McIntosh says: 'America has a great deal of tailored landscape – I like the wildness and the wilderness here, especially in Suffolk. I'm not sure whether I could take the Broads or the Norfolk marshes for ever. What I like so much in Hadleigh is the jumble of styles and details, and the excellence of the polyglot way it's been put together. For me, it lives. For instance, in relation . . . I'm not at all fond of Chelsworth and Lavenham for the very reason that, though they're beautiful to look at, they're like museums. I'd feel uncomfortable living in those two places. Chelsworth is insular, very old, small — they know this themselves; and Lavenham because you couldn't possibly paint your door any other colour than what the Council tells you. They could almost preserve things to death. I like all the funny little mistakes you see in other parts of Suffolk which emphasise that human beings are living there.

'Yes, Hadleigh has changed ever since I began coming in 1961, it's virtually doubled in population. But the new industrial estate was well-sited, well planned, fits in beautifully with the town . . . it sees change yet remains constant. Although I do find a little misplaced antagonism between the town and the estate.'

There was an incident not long ago which made a deep impression on Tom McIntosh's scale of values. He was visited by a television producer in connection with a series of films: 'I took an instant dislike to him because he could only see what he was getting at in terms of his own wittiness and sophistication. Whereas some of the most sophisticated remarks I've heard in terms of perception and shrewdness come from the people I know here . . . for example there's someone living in Kersey running a little shop, and Elsie when she gets going to describe something, her command of English — or Suffolk-English — is superb. She makes something come alive with these lovely phrases and remarks.

'There's something reassuring in all this. Hadleigh's been going for hundreds and hundreds of years, and you feel by God the world may come to grief but Hadleigh will continue to exist. You know, William Dowsing could have been knocking things about and the Civil War was going on, but the characteristics of getting on and getting through always prevailed. It's a natural and realistic way of living . . . still today. There are all the clichés we Americans tend to use about the British muddling through their wars and crises; and it's all true, but there's a kind of steel at the core of the muddle.

'It's home to me now. I don't mean to be lugubrious, but I want to die here in Suffolk. I am American and I'm proud of the country that raised me. It's my heritage and I like it. When I'm in the States some Americans are put off when I say I'm going home to England; they don't approve . . . but that's the way I feel.'

The Journalist: Eric Fowler

Such is the city for which these men, since they disdained to be robbed of it, valiantly fighting have died. And it is fit that every man of you that is left, should be likeminded, to do any travail for the same.

THIS QUOTATION from Pericles headed an article called 'Such is the City' which appeared in the Norwich *Eastern Daily Press* on the morning of 28th July 1949 under the signature of Jonathan Mardle. It is written by a man who has been to war and returned thankfully: 'I cast my mind back to my home thoughts from abroad. When I was homesick for my own city of Norwich, I did not picture to myself the sanitary, spacious, and neatly planned outskirts, nor any municipal institution, admirable though these things are. I thought of the slender tower of the cathedral, and the sturdy towers of the old grey churches, that were built by or for an autocratic priesthood, probably out of what the cant phrase would call the sweat of toiling masses. They recked nothing of expense, and little of threadbare utility, these old builders. They built, as they thought of it, to the glory of God — with an eye to the credit of their sinful selves in the next world.'

The writer seems mesmerised by the past: 'Meanwhile, labourers starved in the hungry 1840's; a little boy named George Edwards started work, crow scaring, at the age of six, and was thrashed for getting drowsy, and his father was sent to prison for stealing turnips to feed his children.' Then to closer times: 'There were still two Englands between the two wars, and the enjoyment of the old, the leisured and the wealthy England was marred for any sensitive man by the miserable consciousness that there were a million of his fellow Englishmen for whom their country had no use, so that their skill, muscle, and character were wasting away in idleness and poverty.'

Bringing his thesis up to date, the writer continues:

'She (England) has put such a responsibility as she never has before into the hands of the common labouring man. He is being trusted to work, and work hard, of his own accord, without the fear of unemployment to drive him to it. It is our greatest experiment in democracy. If it fails, England will collapse.'

It is as if there are two writers, not one. There is the romantic, bereaving an era in which '... no ornament was too lavish ...', and there is the evangelist, issuing threats and warnings about a future which must abandon the frivolous in order to survive.

Eric Fowler, coming home from his own particular war in which he served with the Royal Norfolk Regiment, returned to his old job as a leader writer with the *Eastern Daily Press*. But he wanted to start a gossip column, a request which the editor humoured — provided it involved no payment to outside contributors. Fowler chose his pseudonym Jonathan Mardle (to gossip in Norfolk dialect is to 'mardle'), launching his column in 1946. Instead of a gossip column as such, it became a weekly essay on any subject which caught the author's fancy, not so much about international affairs as parochial goings-on. East Anglia, Norfolk in particular, was Eric Fowler's patch, the place he loved and knew best, and this is what he wrote about.

He wrote about the Norfolk character: 'There's a certain stability in the Norfolker, a great love of county, and this business of what we call "working a steady stroke". We don't make a lot of fuss; we haven't got a lot of time for the sort of man who's known as a ball of fire, who's always showing off. We get the job done, and of course there's a tremendous tradition of conscientious craftsmanship here ... curious thing, when you want to restore a church there are all sorts of craftsmen who'll do it, and love doing it. I think we have contentment. We're reserved and believed, if you like, to exaggerate this local patriotism — you know, East Anglia is the best place under the sun. We're almost instinctively opposed to change ... you see, there's one half of me which would like to put a barbed wire fence round East Anglia to keep the foreigners out. Leave us to pursue the even tenor of our ways. The funny thing is that when these "foreigners" settle down among us, within five years they're more chauvinistic than we are. Yes, there's a lot of Luddite in us . . . and in me.

'The weather has a bit to do with it all — it's responsible for the way we mutter, talk with our mouths shut because we don't want to let this east wind in. Another thing about our characteristics is frugality, a product of 19th century poverty, and in relation to employment it's being mean. There was a paternalism among employers, a willingness to look after their people, to take an interest in their families, but it didn't include paying them any money. It's a tendency that still exists.

'Feudalism? If you like, but those old squires were a darned sight more liberal and fair-minded in their administration than the new generation of bureaucrats dominated by people I would call commuters — they're more harshly Tory than the old squire was. The squire rather shone in adversity as well, whereas the absentee landlord of today is something like a big insurance company which has just bought up tracts of land as an investment. Far from people like the Earl of Leicester at Holkham being chucked out, I think they should be subsidized to run the estate the way they do — they have a sense of duty to the land.'

Eric Fowler was born in Norwich in 1909 and, apart from six years in the army, he has been there ever since. His grandfather was a baker who lived in one of the old streets of the city which were also a 'rich and ripe slum'. The place was 'full of the remains of ancient buildings and some very beautiful 18th century stuff and lots of horrible little slum courts, covered with fleas'. His father was a coal-merchant and the family lived over the shop on the line of the old city wall: 'It was a commodious house. I'm often surprised at the enthusiasm with which local councils are pulling down Victorian terraces, putting up instead modern boxes not half so spacious'. One of five children, Eric Fowler went to Bracondale private school. 'My father had left school when he was 12; like so many men he struggled his way up into a moderately prosperous trade and he wanted nothing to do with any sort of municipal schooling. There were about 90 boys there, a lot of farmers' sons . . . we city boys used to be a bit envious of them — they'd be delivered by their fathers in a pony and trap. No, they weren't conspicuously richer, it was what they did at weekends, because their fathers used to pick them up on the way from market, take them back to the country and we'd hear on Monday tales about the rabbits they'd shot, the pike they'd caught, all the things that were out of reach to us. Our pleasures were of the city, except, don't forget, in those days we could walk from the centre of the city and be in green fields in 10 minutes.

'Every Saturday was this wonderful pageant of Norwich-the-market-town. It was, as now, quite a considerable industrial city, but on a Saturday was the cattle market just below the castle, about six acres . . . well, all the cattle and sheep were driven in. This went on until the beginning of the Second World War. Norwich may have looked like a dignified cathedral city, but on Saturday it became a country town. The streets swarmed with cattle, sheep, drovers . . . a bull in a china shop wasn't just a figure of speech, it really happened.

'How did I become a journalist? Well, that was school. Sad thing, but I had no aptitude for maths or science, and old Williams, the headmaster, was streets ahead of his time in that sort of thing. The other thing was that my father, for reasons best known to himself, retired from his coal business and was foolishly tempted into the boot and shoe trade which he knew nothing about. He went in at the top of a boom at the end of the war, then hit the slump — and his shoe business went bust. He was heartbroken, a terribly conscientious man . . . I watched all these vicissitudes when I was about 12 to 15 and swore I'd never go into business on my own account, I'd seen enough of that — I'd rather someone else did the worrying.

'It wasn't a particularly good time to come out of school in 1925. Father wanted me to go into the coal trade, which I wanted nothing to do with; and the alternative seemed to be a bank — thank God I just missed that one, I very nearly became a bank clerk. Getting into journalism was all due to a schoolmaster, odd old type he was, called Trehearne — came, I believe, from some rather distinguished Cornish family. He had a very high and vivid interest in English literature — he was my first contact with the artistic temperament. But anyway, he was humane enough to go out drinking in the pubs and of course he met the local journalists; and one day he said to me, "Eric, would you like to go on a newspaper?" Well, he took me down to the editor of the *Eastern Daily Press* and I was engaged as an apprentice in the reporters' room, passing rich at about 15 bob a week — and that was that.'

But not quite that for, as we have seen, Eric became a leader writer and then a columnist. 'Inspiration? It wasn't inspiration at all — it was perspiration and desperation, the feeling "my God" on Tuesday that the printers will want Jonathan Mardle by five o'clock, I'd better write something.'

Write something he did, his choice being, to say the least, eclectic: one week it would be a dissertation on being shampooed by his barber — 'if he did not shampoo my head my hair would fall out — or so he says.' Next week he might discuss the poetry of Bernard Barton, the Quaker poet of Woodbridge; or then again he might reminisce about his army service — 'I did not look the part, neither could I think myself into it. I acted it as best I could, but I fear I was a ham actor and a bad soldier.' On another occasion he would philosophise on the effect of a carol service — 'it was not everybody's idea of religion. It is possible to write the whole thing off as moonshine — a precious and sentimental attempt to revive the Age of Faith by assuming its trappings. A materialist would call it childish and superstitious. Yet it was beautiful and spiritual.'

Whatever subject he tackled, his approach was down to earth; rarely was he given to flights of fancy, never to purple prose; if his style was not lean and taut in, say, the manner of a Hemingway, neither was it fulsome and flowery. He has always taken the Norfolk way, working a steady stroke: 'I'm sorry to say it was very much the shallow end; I didn't fancy myself as an authority on what happened the other side of the world. A lot of it — I started at Easter 1946 — was concerned with the sheer delight that the war was over and I was back home again. The first thing I wrote was about Castle Mound in the middle of Norwich — there was Norwich, really shabby at that time, shattered in parts by bombs, but there in the middle of it was this beautiful green mound covered every Easter with daffodils.

'Message? Well, if there was a message it's something I've tried to put over from that day to this — by casting my mind back to the way things were before the war; the thing that I rejoice in and which also grieves me is that we just don't know how well off we've been and still are. If you face the facts, the 19th century had been impoverished in East Anglia; it was all governed by farm wages which were the rock bottom of any wages. The towns were depressed as well, because the only alternative was farming, so town people were just as badly paid . . . I think the chap who first talked to me about these modern changes of the late 1950's was Eldon Griffiths, M.P. for Bury St. Edmunds. He said to me, "There's an industrial revolution coming, so let's make it a civilized revolution" — and that's the cry I took up. I think we've got the chance to avoid some of the mistakes they made in the north of England and the Midlands in the late 18th and early 19th centuries.

'Yes, I am optimistic about the future. I don't think one can afford to be pessimistic; and every time I catch myself moaning — as old men do — I just look back and think about the slums behind the beautiful Georgian streets of towns like Aylsham. And you think of the state of country cottages . . . thatched roofs may have looked picturesque, but they were damp, cold, unhealthy. You know, before the war T.B. was rife in country areas. We had an enlightened Medical Officer of Health who said: "We can't afford to send our consumptives to Switzerland, but I'll get the County Council to make little revolving shelters which consumptives can put in their gardens to live in for the open air treatment at home and to prevent them infecting their families." We used to call it the White Scourge, it was so prevalent.

'Something else, I had a trip to America in 1956 and the thing that struck me in that great land of opportunity was that I saw more beggars in my first day in New York than I'd seen in England since the end of the war. In the 1920's there was a regular row of beggars in what we call the Back of the Inns of Norwich; there were children with irons on their legs to try to correct rickets. There was simply bad malnutrition. They were producing food they were too poor to buy.

'Then there was the agricultural depression. I saw it going round the country as a reporter, the pasture degenerating into scrub, fences growing 20 feet high because no one could afford to do the hedges, farm buildings and cottages falling into dilapidation. You can't blame the farmers entirely. There's always been the economic assumption in this country, probably since the Repeal of the Corn Laws, that food must be cheap. The principle of life here was to get food in the cheapest possible market in order that the industrial production should be down as steeply as possible in the lowest possible wages. The result was of course that prices reached rock bottom. I used to see the wretched farmers going round the Corn Hall in Norwich from merchant to merchant after harvest, and half the merchants wouldn't even look at them.

'The tide started to change in 1937-ish, but it was the war that changed the situation radically. Farming always prospers in a war; and praise God this time the salvation was continued food shortage afterwards and that great Minister of Agriculture in Attlee's government, Tom Williams, who introduced guaranteed prices.

'I think that even so, farm workers are more faithful to their labour than townpeople — it's in the towns that discontent festers. We, according to some left wingers, are sinfully contented around here... Norwich has always been accused of being hellishly complacent.'

If one claimed that Jonathan Mardle is the city's conscience, it might equally be reasoned that he is its Devil's Advocate. The Luddite or the penitent Luddite?

The Blind Man: Jim Goodliffe

AT 5.20 pm on 29th March 1967 Jim Goodliffe and his 18 year old son, John, emerged from Park Royal underground station. On holiday in London, they were returning to their Ealing friends, the Thomases, after visiting the Industrial Design Centre exhibition in Haymarket. Turning left into Corringway, they headed along the left hand pavement towards number 12.

At 5.25 pm, as they passed number 110, a learner driver, approaching on the other side of the road, drew out to overtake another car. The learner swerved to the right, lost control, mounted the opposite pavement, knocking down Jim Goodliffe.

When he came to several days later in the Royal Middlesex Hospital, Jim Goodliffe's first recollection is of being fed by a nurse. He could not understand why the ward was so dark, imagining a new kind of rest therapy. It was not therapy: in the accident Jim's optic nerve had been severed, leaving him totally blind. The learner driver, illegally at the wheel, because he was unaccompanied, was fined £32 by a magistrate's court; his provisional licence was suspended for six months.

Jim Goodliffe was 46 years old at the time. After a war in the R.N.V.R., during which he had married a WREN, he eventually became group secretary for the National Farmers' Union. After his release from hospital he would not admit to his blindness: 'It's a fairly common defense mechanism, I believe.' It was not until June, feeling the warmth of the sun on his face, yet seeing nothing, that he accepted the fact. He also faced the reality of keeping his family together on £7. 15s. a week health benefit.

In October 1967, the Goodliffes settled into a suburban villa in Woodlark Road, Cambridge. Jim found temporary work as appeals organiser with the Royal National Institute for the Blind, at the same time instigating legal action for compensation. At the end of five years to-ing and fro-ing, the case was heard before the High Court. In his wisdom, the judge assessed the price of Jim Goodliffe's darkness at £45,000.

Shortly after he lost his sight, Jim Goodliffe started to learn braille from a local blind teacher. He began gathering tips about how to feel his way with a white stick. In November 1967 he went to the RNIB Queen Elizabeth Home at Torquay for a 12 weeks' course: braille, touch typing, the long cane method of mobility; shortly afterwards he was taking his first steps away from home.

'I had been self-pitying — a despicable thing. So I determined to make the most of things as they were, not as I'd like them to be. Get rid of wishful thinking . . . a conscious effort. Push forward to find your limitations and you'll be surprised to see how far off they are. Of course I got lost. Once I turned into someone's garage, thinking it was a street corner and couldn't get out.

'I still get lost, even a quarter of a mile from here. We're very vulnerable . . . I learned that from a blind friend who was walking his guide dog on Parker's Piece. He let the dog off to have a run and sat on the grass. A beggar asked him for money and my friend explained that he was a blind old age pensioner who couldn't afford to give money away. The beggar said he wasn't blind — he didn't have a stick, that he was just a mean bastard. Then he spat in my friend's face. My friend was angry and wanted to hit the beggar, but he couldn't — he didn't know where he was. So he wiped the spit from his face and carried on with his day.

'Blindness has taken a lot of hate out of my life. You can't hate . . . that makes you even more vulnerable.'

Jim Goodliffe is five foot eight, fit, knowing exactly where you are and looking — or so it seems — directly into your eyes. His movements are sure. He could not seem less helpless. Of his blindness Jim says: 'I'm more disappointed than sorry: I would like to have done so much more — but the old self-pity has gone.' His wife, Mary, admits that there is a feeling of sadness in her which never quite goes. She is a very gentle person, grateful when Jim does things for her, when he washes up. She says that he used, before the accident, to be a retiring, bookish person. Today he is an extrovert — she has seen the change.

Their future? 'I'm quite sure they'll learn to join

nerves — that's the difficult thing, *joining nerves.* I'm convinced they'll do it and that I'll see again.'

The past plays an important part in a blind person's life. He is drawn in upon himself more than most, particularly in cases where blindness struck after years of sight; he is bound to review in his mind's eye yesterday's images. In a way he is an emotional hermit, sitting in a perpetually darkened room, re-running old movies time and time again. It is both his life's pleasure and tragedy.

'My father,' Jim Goodliffe recalls, 'was a grocer in St. Ives. I went to the local grammar school — St. Ives was the ideal place to be a boy. We had fields, a river . . . I learned to swim in it, boat on it, fall in it, fish in it. It was all I wanted.'

After school came years in the merchant navy, sailing the world, yet conscious that he was missing something. 'There were blue skies in the tropics, but I missed walking and I missed live things, like birds. I remember the first time I came back — I was amazed at how green England was. Cambridgeshire as I remember it was a country of trees — elms in particular, elms and ashes, wonderful hedgerows, blackthorn, long grass and hedge parsley in great white clouds. Mind you, this was long before they cut the grass by the roadside. A fine picture it made to me. And plum blossom — you don't think much about plum blossom, but it was like snow on the trees. I remember once driving back to Cambridge from the Midlands. There was a beautiful smell of hay in the air, and I'd only smelt smoke and grime where I'd come from. But my finest memory is of the sky, the cloud formations, with trees beneath . . . we don't have landscapes broken by hills and mountains, not much drama, but it's green. Really, East Anglia as I remember seeing it was parkland. Yes, I can see it sharply.'

In *Grantchester,* Rupert Brooke was acid about Cambridge people who were, he wrote, 'urban, squat and packed with guile'. 'Oh, I think he was having a bit of fun because I could aim most of his anti-Cambridge invective against Grantchester if I tried . . . no, it's not a village where I feel at home. It's a place that shuts its front doors to me. I've always had my best fun in the fenland villages running from Fen Drayton, Swavesey, Over, Willingham, Cottenham — flat and dull if you like, but it's the people.

They've got character, they're really in the soil, they grew from the soil, their livelihood depends on the soil — unfriendly, yes. To go back to Brooke: "at Over they fling oaths at one . . . and worse than oaths at Trumpington".

'I think country people felt that Cambridge people looked a bit down on them. It was a town versus country attitude. There was a lot of bureaucracy. I remember a councillor saying to me that if they made any more regulations, you'd need to put up barbed wire to keep Cambridge people in and country folk out. Country people felt that both town and gown had little time for them. My last sighted memories of Cambridge are of grey stone walls, the Backs in Spring, and quite a lot of flowers . . . and bicycles. As a boy I could always pick out the undergrads, even without their gowns — they were tidier . . . they were a cut above the rest of us, probably because they washed regularly and we didn't.

'We weren't envious. It was taken as their right. They were public school boys; but I dare say we could have got there if we'd tried hard enough and were good enough. I was never brought up to think of class and money, but of course we were on a sort of social treadmill. You wanted to go up, not down. We were taught you don't go down, there's plenty of room at the top, so get there. Today? The undergraduates don't seem to have the polish. There's no longer a University accent as I think there used to be.'

Jim 'sees' different characteristics as he moves around the country. (He uses the word 'sees' as a sighted person does: 'Looking forward to seeing you,' he says on the telephone). 'I used to be able to tell which village a man came from. Up by Willingham and Cottenham there's a sing-song tune comes into the voice and it's a little nasal, tends to get softer the further south you go — and as you go east it turns into the slower, more measured Suffolk accent. But if a Cambridgeshire man differs from the rest he generally remains an East Anglian at heart.

'If I could open my eyes today I feel I'd see more traffic; more people, more tourists and foreigners. We used to have a quiet time between October and Easter, now there are always hundreds of tourists. I sense that the carefree attitude has gone, people seem so intent, frenzied — but this could be purely imagination.'

What is not imagination is the change in certain social

patterns and orders. Jim Goodliffe has his hair cut at Joshua Taylor, walking the two miles home unaided. He uses his long white cane which he sweeps before him to left and right — a veritable mine-detector — walking at the same pace as a sighted person. The stick tapping gives 'echoes' of varying tremor, so that he can tell whether it is a brick wall or wooden fence he is following; knowing by the same system when he reaches a corner. There are certain blind-man's codes: 'If you run into a lampost, make sure it's an aluminium one. They have rounded edges; concrete ones have sharp edges.' He recites the names of the shops he passes, although 'the names are 11 years old, so they've probably changed.'

'Joshua Taylor used to advertise in one of their windows that they had 12 barber's chairs, so you could just go in and get your hair cut at once. Now you've got to make an appointment. I think it's to do with personal service, people seem almost ashamed to serve these days. I suppose it's another manifestation of what's acceptable and what's not acceptable — the countryman feels that the man working in an office block in a hot-house atmosphere must be a bit odd. And vice versa. It's the countryman's attitude to anyone not doing what he's doing, a pitying attitude — except in mid-winter, then he might be grudgingly envious. Then again, it's all a bit confused today because Cambridge has lots of newcomers — commuters — who spend half their lives in London; so Cambridge is really three cities now: town, gown and commuter.'

Permitted one single memory of his sighted days, Jim reverts to the countryside, a countryside he still explores on a tandem bicycle with Adrian Moult, a sixth former from Leys School. 'I can visualise it, you see. I knew it before. For my memory I'd have to choose elm trees. They're threatened . . . and as a boy I watched the seasons in a particular elm: the first bit of green, to full leaf and then the yellow sheen as it came into flower, then the falling of the seed afterwards. I've heard the wind rustling in it and I've seen the snow settling on it and I had a real affection for that elm.

'It's a proud tree. Like the East Anglian perhaps — he's pretty proud. Perhaps that's what I meant by attitudes to service . . . I think that the East Anglian character wouldn't breed a good race of head waiters.'

* * * * * *

There are more than 118,000 blind people residing in this country; approximately one in 500 of the population. Each year more than 12,000 lose their sight. Put another way, in Britain someone goes blind every 43 minutes.

The Trawlerman: Harry Blowers

TO GIVE HIM full due, it is 'Skipper H.G. Blowers, M.B.E.'. Member of the British Empire . . . it is a winter's story, a story of valour. Newspaper cuttings record the events of that winter of 1965. Newspaper cuttings, and a silver cup inscribed upon the base of which is the citation: 'Presented by Her Majesty's Government to H.G. Blowers skipper of motor trawler *St. Martin* in recognition of his skill and seamanship in rendering assistance to m.t. *Bermuda* on 2nd to 3rd November 1965 and to m.t. *Kingfish* on 30th November to 2nd December 1965.'

The Queen presented Harry Blowers with his medal at a Buckingham Palace investiture: 'I was a bit apprehensive. It said on the card "Dress suit preferred", so I went to Moss Bros to hire a tail coat and tall hat. Never worn one before and never worn one since. I was more nervous collecting that medal than earning it. I'm hard of hearing, see? And I didn't expect the Queen to actually speak to me — when she did I was flabbergasted. She asked me what I did, I heard that. So I told her I was a fisherman. Then she asked me something else, but I missed it. That embarrassed me. She shook my hand and moved on . . . a very fine lady.'

'Rendering assistance' has a touch of understatement. *Bermuda* and *Kingfish* had engine trouble; Harry Blowers towed them back to Lowestoft Harbour: 'The *Bermuda* wasn't too much trouble. The *Kingfish* was different. The line parted, see? Well, it was getting dark, so we laid on broadside, thinking we'd pick up in the morning. But I just couldn't sleep. Something kept telling me I'd have to pick up before daylight or I wouldn't do it at all. I told the mate and he said you can't do that, it's pitch dark — but I knew we had to. Call the crew out, I said, and we'll try to pick him up. First time we missed. Second time we got him. Then the snow came, snow and a force 12 hurricane. We were blinded. Ten minutes more and we'd have been too late. Made me think, that did. I don't do a lot of praying, but I said the Lord's Prayer to myself then. Something just told me . . . makes you think, doesn't it?'

Harry first went to sea at nine. That was for a joy ride. In 1917 he signed on as cook at the age of 13. 'Why? I don't know why. I liked the sea. My father was a trawler skipper, so I joined his crew. There was nothing else in Lowestoft in those days — fishing *was* Lowestoft, you could smell fish everywhere. There were about 200 trawlers then, 60 to 80 feet long. We were a sailing smack with a crew of five. The skipper got £1 a week, the mate 18s., two deck hands 12s. each and the cook 10 bob. We used to go out for eight to 10 days in the North Sea, trawling for plaice, soles, dabs, brill . . . ground fish.

'All depended on the weather. No wind, no sailing, no fish. A good haul would be 10 to 12 baskets, a bad haul 10 to 12 fish. It was rare to make a good living. And how we worked. The cook worked from 6 am 'til 8.30pm, but we ate well — fried fish breakfast, roast meat dinner, plenty of tea and cocoa. It was hard; conditions were bad. Seven hours stood on deck in a snow storm, that's hard. Some got frostbite. Sometimes there was a man overboard, but never on my boat. You could say I was lucky.

'No toilets. You went over the side or in a bucket on deck, and you usually slept damp — you pulled your blanket right over your head so that it trapped your breath. That's how you kept warm. We'd come back after our 10 days, land the fish, scrub out, take on ice and be off again, 24 hours later, seven days a week. Holidays? Let me see now — we married in 1924 and we took our first holiday in 1934. We went to London, but we didn't think much of that — everyone was in such a hurry. Holiday was unemployment, and you dreaded that. Real holidays were unknown in the fishing trade.'

Harry Blowers and his wife live in Winnipeg Road, a street of turn-of-the-century villas. The sea is not far away, but you cannot see it. Their three children have grown up and moved away from home, so there is plenty of space for the upright piano whose keyboard is seldom touched. There is a ship in a bottle, a Toby jug, arrangements of plastic flowers, a plate of mint-humbugs next to Harry's medicine. He does not always feel well these days and complains that he has dropped from 14 stone to under 10 stone since he retired in 1968.

'I've no regrets... except about being greedy. I stayed on too long. I mean, I was 63 at the time of the *Bermuda* and *Kingfish* business. Should've stopped while I could enjoy being retired. Now I can't get used to it. There's not much to enjoy ashore... things got better when I had my own trawler. The *Cordelia* she was, and I was 23. Another sailing smack of 24 tons, open deck, no wheelhouse, just a tiller, one cabin below, engine room for the steam capstan, sails store and fish holds. Everything got better — I was always in the top 10 for landings every year. My best year paid £3,700. Today young skippers make £10,000 to £12,000. Floating palaces, four star hotels they are with their toilets and showers and separate cabins.

'You were a team years ago. Your life was in the next man's hands and his in yours. You went through hell together, then the weather cleared, the sun came out and you were happy. It was quiet, just the sails and creaking, the boom banging about. You were alone. I was never really happy ashore — I'd get restless and want to go back to the sea. It's just that I was happier. It was terrible leaving, but I've got used to it. Well, that's what I tell myself... but sometimes I don't believe what I tell myself.

'The navigational aids they have today! We had a sextant and instinct — fish mostly set in on a growing moon, and you learnt where the grounds were. They have all sorts of fancy toys today — we had the North Star and a lead line 30 fathoms long. You put a blob of grease on the lead so it picked up sand, and you knew where you were from the specks in the sand. Floating palaces and people dodging work today! Still, I'd go back if I was young. Couldn't have worked in an office, sitting at a desk. The sea — well, it smells good. They say that fishermen and farm workers are a different breed. Don't you believe it. They're the same — they both know how to stand on their own two feet. They're workers. We knew it in our blood, we knew that we worked or we'd starve. Simple as that.'

Harry Blowers has a full head of white hair, unruly hair. His hands are long and slender, an artist's hands more than a seaman's. He seems troubled, says that he will be 76, 'if I make it'. He rocks slightly as he talks, occasionally doubling up at the waist as if in pain; but if this is the case it does not show in his face. He is given to long moments of silence, suddenly withdrawing from talk, lowering his head in excommunication. At such times you need to be patient because he is lost, a thousand miles away in private reverie. Then, when he is ready, his head jerks up and he continues where he left off. His eyes are set deep in a rather gaunt face; they are penetrating eyes.

'Pity I'm not too good today. The doctor's coming. We could've gone down to the fish market, the harbour . . . seen who was there. Could've talked to some of them. I get short of breath if I walk far. Not much equipped for walking am I?' He gestures towards his feet which are clad in woolly bedroom slippers.

Mrs. Blowers: 'He doesn't get enough exercise – just sits. It's good that he's ashore . . . I used to worry in the gales. You could hear that wind scream and I knew he was out there. When he retired he kept wandering off. Be gone for hours and hours. Then I discovered where he'd been. Down to the harbour and the market, looking for friends. Couldn't keep away. Now he just sits.'

* * * * * *

Bermuda and *Kingfish* are both in harbour, tied up to the dock broadside. They are taking on food, ice is being shovelled into the holds. They do not seem like floating palaces, these sturdy, pugnacious vessels, with rust clotting like dried blood upon their plates. At the market radios blare and knives are slitting, gutting; boxes are packed, loaded into vans – H.W. Cladingbowl, Fish Merchant; W.E. Scrivener, Fish Merchant. At the Europa Canteen, 'Proprietress Mrs L.K. Hunter', the tea is sweet, strong, scalding. The sea looks truculent.

A bit of company would be welcome. Someone who knows the ropes. Someone like Harry Blowers, M.B.E. But Harry has left the sea; he has come in from the cold. He is sitting in Winnipeg Road, waiting for the doctor to call, wearing bedroom slippers and sucking mint-humbugs to take away the taste of the medicine.

The Parson: The Reverend Charles Cowley

MANY OF THE SOULS within his cure call Charles Cowley the One Arm Bandit; to others he is known as the Bionic Priest — a sobriquet which stuck after a sermon for which he drew as his text the exhortation *'If thy right hand offend thee, cut it off.'* With which he detached his artificial right arm, flinging it down the aisle. His church is packed like Sunday Night at the Palladium and, so far as one can see, Mr. Cowley is loved by saint and sinner.

When he was quite young his arm was sliced off in a mixing machine in London, Ontario. 'We were working on an interesting biscuit recipe,' he recalls. It turned out to be a sublime illustration of the mysterious way in which God moves: the biscuit mix was blessed with an original protein flavour, while the compensation awarded to Charles Cowley paid his theological college fees.

The Vicar of Aldringham and Thorpeness is an eccentric — and no other parson would do for his parish. He is, ever so slightly, out of step with the times; which is just as well, because Aldringham and Thorpeness — particularly Thorpeness — are mightily out of step with the times.

Let us begin at the beginning. In 1911 Thorpeness was a 'mud hole with one tree'. Then Glencairn Stuart Ogilvie, who had inherited the estate a few years earlier, conceived a dream of turning the place into a private holiday village. A company 'Seaside Bungalows' — later to become 'Thorpeness Ltd' — was registered, and building started. And such building... the weirdest assembly of follies it is possible to imagine. Intended originally to be Tudor, the construction followed Mr. Ogilvie's dictum that his village should be 'for people who want to experience life as it was lived when England was Merrie England'. Thorpeness remained in the Ogilvie family until the company went into voluntary liquidation in March 1977. It was, says George Cook, who worked for the Ogilvies for 52 years, 'benevolent paternalism... they were God's gentlemen!'

Benevolent, paternal or whatever, there was no getting away from it that, once completed, Thorpeness was a freak. One cottage, known as the House in the Clouds, is 100 ft. high and, in addition to living accommodation, contains two water tanks which supplied the village. A breathlessly admiring Ogilvie holiday in Venice resulted in a Venetian street in Thorpeness. Netherlands is the name of another group of houses; there is a neo-Norman gateway; Swiss chalets co-exist with Tudorbethan; and there is a 90 acre mere or lake dotted with islands named after J.M. Barrie's characters ... the Ogilvies retaining affectionate memories of *Peter Pan.*

In 1914 Thorpeness was unveiled to a rather bemused press. *The Times,* with rapturous ambiguity, remarked: 'Thorpeness possesses no attraction for the tripper ... visitors make their own amusements and sport like butterflies in the brisk air beneath the joyous sun, amid surroundings as unlike those of an ordinary British seaside resort as it is possible to imagine.'

The astonishing thing about the entire business is that it *worked.* Middle class families rented the seven or eight bedroom houses all summer long, packing off nannies and charges to the 'Juvenilia' while the grown ups biffed small white balls over the golf course, drank modern American cocktails in the turreted club house, entered tennis tournaments at the Country Club. Children sailed, canoed, punted or floated ecstatically on the mere and there was never a drowning accident (to this very day) because at no point is the water deeper than three feet. There was – and is – a Beware of Crocodile sign, but everyone knows that the wretched beast is only after Captain Hook.

The summers were endless, Herr Hitler was merely a ranting politician the other side of the channel and, on the evening of 28th August 1926 at the Regatta '... chinese lanterns of vivid hues swaying slightly in the breeze enhanced the beauty of the effect ... an air of jollity was maintained until the early hours.' Thus commented the *Leiston Observer.*

Then something very odd happened. Someone stopped the clock. And no one has ever rewound it. Thorpeness has become petrified within the fabric of its yesterdays. It is still *Beano, Dandy,* and *Hotspur* country;

Biggles is read by the young, Michael Arlen by the adults; Oxford bags are in vogue. Joan Hunter-Dunn plays strenuous sets, volleying as she has never volleyed before, and there are echoes of 'well played!' Such is the hallucination.

Albert-the-boatman has been looking after the children three generations now, since 1928: 'No, it's much the same. Things don't change much. I was teaching their grandfathers to row.' Eric Hawes has been tennis pro at the Country Club for more than 20 years, sharing his time between Thorpeness and Charterhouse: 'It's a sort of public-school-on-sea here ... we try to teach them to be good losers on court — etiquette, if you like. Even in my time I remember coaching Mrs. Harewood-Smith when she was Miss Caroline. Everyone knows each other and have done as families for years. No one complains ... well, one doesn't, does one?' Charles Cowley: 'It's the wrong kind of soil here for harvesting crime.'

At the centre of it all is the Country Club, all chintz, with wicker tables and chairs on the veranda over the tennis courts. The bedrooms are not the most luxurious in the land and the lounge bar is exactly like the inside of a tennis pavilion — high rafters, team photographs, shields upon the walls. Notice boards list tomorrow's matches and, until quite recently, black ties were worn for dinner, after which the orchestra played daring foxtrots. The food is wholesome, the water hot, the guest list implacably middle class. And no one complains, even if the water isn't hot. Well, one doesn't, does one?

In the evening there are general knowledge quizzes and housey housey (no, not bingo which is *quite* different), and teenagers dance those thump-thump dances so that the whole wooden building shakes. There are barbeques in the grounds and late night swimming parties in the pool, but if you are due on court at eight thirty in the morning, then eight thirty it is.

Without the Club, there would be little else: just one shop — The Shop — a pub called The Dolphin, the alms houses; and that is about the lot. A bus occasionally connects Thorpeness with the outside world, entering a kind of emotional passport control as it reaches the village. Such is the parish, or at least a large part of it, of the Reverend Charles Cowley.

Aldringham Vicarage is Victorian, utilitarian rather than architecturally distinguished. The Vicar's study is first on the right and the telephone never stops ringing, Charles Cowley loping up and down, cradling the instrument in his good arm, trailing the specially lengthened cord in his wake. The telephone is of the push-button variety, the post office insisting that he should have it at no extra charge because he kept breaking the dialling mechanism with his tin arm — he is pleased about that. 'I like the 'phone,' he says, 'it's a very private means of communication.' He does everything jerkily, as if his strings are operated by a not terribly efficient marionette master. He smokes a cigarette jerkily, forgetting where he has put it down; he talks jerkily, flying off at tangents; he even hums jerkily.

He is absent-minded, occasionally calling marriage banns more times than tradition prescribes. The name 'Michael Watkins' is scrawled across a page in his diary in multiples and at odd angles, reminding him that he broke the previous appointment. A white crucifix hangs above the fireplace, an Emwood cartoon from a wall, vestments from a hook on the door. Above his desk is an Ordnance Survey of his parish; in one corner of the map is a sticker quoting — probably not from the scriptures — 'Warm massage is the answer to your problem'.

'This is the time,' he explains, 'between nine and 10, when I stay at my desk to plan the day. People know they can reach me. Also, when you're ordained you undertake to say prayers morning and evening, so I do it here, together with the day's reading . . . oh good, it's a nice one today from St. John — you know, about it being expedient that one man should die for the people rather than that a nation should be destroyed.'

He reads, isolating himself, drawing silence around him like a cloak . . . until the telephone intrudes. Someone in need of spiritual comfort: '. . . yes, I see — yes, the epistles talk about *the* life, *the* truth, but it only becomes personal when you apply love to it . . . the Church of England is a marvellous piece of machinery, a splendid vehicle . . . well, yes I think of God in a hopelessly inexplicable way . . .'

At 10 o'clock he leaves his desk, clutching at an *aide-memoire*. In the drive is a Ford Popular: 'It was given to me by an 85 years' old parishioner who'd run it until he was told not to drive any more — I believe it was made in 1950, but it goes terribly well. You won't mind coming in it, will you?' Surprisingly, it starts first go; Charles Cowley engages gear with the smoothness of a medieval siege. He seems unaware of the grating noise. He presses the horn as we move through the vicarage gates, but there is a malfunction.

'I was brought up a Roman Catholic, but somehow I couldn't accept the dogma, so I was more or less automatically excommunicated, after which I converted. My belief has always been a bit unconventional and I somehow just felt that I might be of use to people with the same feelings. They said at my interview when I applied for ordination that my views were a little mystical, but they went along with it . . . I say, can you smell a sort of hot smell? My goodness, I do believe there's no water in this car.'

He nurses it along at five miles an hour to an Aldeburgh garage where, at the touch of the radiator cap, a geyser of steam leaps into the air. The mechanic, with the look of a man who has been there before, refills the radiator. The vicar gives another soundless toot on the horn and aims for Aldeburgh beach where he scrunches across the shingle to talk to John, a fisherman, about the crab hauls and whether oil spillage is affecting the catches. The sea is running high, hurling pebbles on to the shore with each wave.

'Oh, I accept the creed absolutely, its whole mystery makes sense to me. Jesus knew he came from somewhere else, he knew he was *the* son of God . . . what he was teaching is that we can all be sons of God.'

He stops the Popular outside the Jubilee Hall, scene of Britten's first concerts in the Aldeburgh Festival. 'I thought we might pick up a few cheap chairs at the sale for the church hall; we can't afford new ones and you can sometimes get them for about £1 here.' The chairs are down as lot 42, so he jerks off down the street to see the church organist, jerking back into the sale in time to bid. The chairs are knocked down to the opposition for £10 apiece: 'Well, we can't compete with that . . . where was I? Oh yes, it's a small parish here, about 1,200, so it's not the usual job of baptisms, weddings, funerals, Sunday School,

Mothers' Union — 90% of my job is visiting, talking to people, human contact. I talk to them, not as a priest or philosopher but as a friend — about housing, jobs, illness. It's them that bring up God, not me — then it gives us a chance to discuss; but it's not teaching so much as interpreting life, interpreting what they feel already. Take falling in love — don't you think that's a marvellous manifestation of the divine spark? I'd chuck it all and do something else along similar lines if I was directed to a city parish. I couldn't do it any more than I could become an astronaut.'

Aldeburgh Cottage Hospital is next on his list, 17 beds in all and a quick look around to see if any of his parishioners are there. A word with Sister and another with Dr. Ian Tait; a longer chat with Charlie Miller, the newsagent, who has had a spot of heart trouble and who says, in an aside, 'He gives us a lift, Charles does.' The Bionic Priest calls everyone by first name; they call him Charles.

The Popular rattles along the sea road joining Aldeburgh to Thorpeness: 'The life I was leading before all this was meaningless to me — so this became the only thing to do . . . I don't know why. No, I don't have doubts. If I did I'd have to chuck it as well; but I don't. As I said, I'm not a dogmatist, dogma can get in the way. Basically, I say I don't know, I don't know what it's all about, it's a discovering process.'

In Thorpeness there is Percy Westrup to see. Percy is a retired fisherman who made all the curtains in his cottage in the way he made fishing nets, each knot a perfect knot. There is a *Daily Mail World War Two Map* on one wall, a colour photograph of his wife's grave on another. There is no talk of God or church or services between Percy and Charles, only the have-a-cup-of-tea talk of friends.

One more call, to see George Marling, church warden, about repairs to the roof; then it is time for half a pint of beer at the Dolphin. It is hard for those at the bar to buy Charles a drink because he insists on buying them a drink and hates to take no for an answer.

Still there is time to look in at his church of St. Andrew, ancient of foundation but heavily and none too prettily restored in the last century. Yet the churchyard is lovely, clear, open, far from the hubbub of the living. A plain cross is marked 'In loving memory of Joshua Chard, the Suffolk hero, found drowned on Thorpe Beach Dec. 21 1875 aged 63 years'. A mass of visitors come to see him, remarks Charles . . . and a mass come to Holy Communion and Matins each Sunday, filling quite regularly every one of the 100 places in the church. And that can't be bad. Mind you, in summer — when tennis is next to godliness — Sunday tournaments are timed not to start until Matins are over, Charles and the officiating umpire reaching a tacit compromise between the needs of body and soul. So tennis whites brighten the congregation and rackets are stowed beneath pews and Fight the Good Fight is sung with feeling.

'If there's life after death, then I believe there must also be life before birth. I regard life as a small part of the process. I mean, perhaps we might be posted to Uganda or somewhere awful — but it's all a means to an end. I cannot believe that it is all an accident; that would be terrible and pointless . . . it would be like saying I'm dreaming. You know what Descartes wrote: *"Cogito, ergo sum."* I think, therefore I am.

'I met a man a while ago who'd been through Nazi concentration camp and tortured in the most unbelievable way. He said to me, "Death is nothing." But what about life, I asked him. You know what he said? He said, "Life? It's a single hour in the schoolroom." '

The Landowner: Lord Tollemache

IN THE GREAT PARK at Helmingham stand two particular oak trees. They are only feet apart, their branches reaching towards each other in the way of comrades, roots thrusting deep into Suffolk soil. Their trunks are massive, gnarled, contorted. One has been torn apart at the heart, perhaps by lightning; you could almost drive a car into the cavity. Miraculously, the wound healed and the tree lives on, shedding leaves in autumn, budding each spring.

These trees were already five centuries old when brave Hal led his troops to victory at Agincourt. They had reached their first growth when Canute was king of England. Tests have shown that they were planted at about the time of the Viking pillage of our East Anglian shores.

Still they stand, with stamina yet for another four or five hundred years; and the view from beneath the canopy of their foliage has changed little over the ages. The park is as virgin as ever it was, untouched by plough since at least Tudor times. Red deer and fallow deer roam at will, shy of strangers to this day. Highland cattle chew the cud and soay sheep graze a green and pleasant land, overlooked by the house where the Tollemaches of Helmingham have lived since 1487.

Neither was this the beginning, for the Tollemache family, probably originating in Normandy, have absolute ties with Suffolk since 1180. The main family seat became Bentley, near Ipswich, until in 1487 John Tollemache married Elizabeth Joyce of Helmingham. Their son, Lionel, also married a Joyce, cementing the union further; and Helmingham became, and has remained since, the principal home of the Tollemaches.

The house in 1487 was called Creke Hall and stood on the site of the present Hall; indeed portions of the older house can still be seen incorporated inside Helmingham; but by 1510 the new Hall had been completed by Lionel Tollemache in traditional half-timbered Tudor style, with an overhang both around the outside and inside the courtyard. Apart from exterior changes it is almost exactly the same to this day and most of the chimneys are original.

The main exterior changes were the removal of the Tudor gables, with the exception of the corner ones, about 1760 when, together with other Georgian alterations, the existing half-timbered walls were covered with the present tiles on the front aspect. In 1800 the architect Nash covered these over on the instructions of Wilbraham Tollemache, 6th Earl of Dysart, who thought that grey stucco and battlements would make Helmingham more of a castle ... fortunately, aesthetic taste superseded bellicose sentiments, the stucco being removed in 1821.

Helmingham has been lucky over the centuries because whenever the Hall was in danger of falling into disrepair, a later generation came along to rebuild and restore their family home. Thus it was in the case of the 1st Lord Tollemache who, on his succession in 1840, found the place in a deplorable state. Just over a hundred years later the 4th Lord Tollemache found the Hall sadly neglected: no electricity, no bathrooms, drinking water taken from the moat.

So, like the oaks in the park, like the Tollemaches themselves, Helmingham Hall has seen bad days as well as good. Stately homes do not remain stately by divine providence; the fabric of their existence is maintained by dedication, by sweat, by love.

Timothy John Edward is the 5th Lord Tollemache, inheriting on the death of his father in 1975. Born in 1939, he was educated at Eton, from where he joined the army, being commissioned into the Coldstream Guards to serve in Kenya and the Persian Gulf. Leaving the regiment, he took a course in estate management at Sandringham, after which he became a trainee at Barings Bank until he joined the family business of Tollemache and Cobbold Breweries in Ipswich in 1965. In 1970 he married; he and his wife have a daughter and a son. His recreations are shooting, fishing, natural history; his clubs, White's, Pratt's, Boodle's.

These are the facts, the pedigree, open for all to see who care to lift *Who's Who* from the library shelf. Like passport photographs, they tell one very little about the subject: two ears, a nose geographically located where noses usually are . . . not much else. The facts portray an Identikit 39 year old peer of the realm.

To actually *know* Lord Tollemache is another matter, because he is a very private person. He defends his privacy in the way that Helmingham's moat defends his home. He permits us to know precisely as much as he wants us to know about him before lowering his emotional portcullis; it is a device most Englishmen employ as a means of self-protection. Reservation is implicit in our nature.

From certain viewpoints in a world of clever modern men this attitude is considered a quaint anachronism, a dodo moving immutably towards extinction. The truth may be that the Englishman himself does not know exactly what he is — or care much for that matter. He is not given to long periods of self-examination, tending to get pink about the ears and incoherent when put to inquisition. Television has largely abandoned the 'Excuse me, sir, are you a dodo moving immutably towards extinction?' technique of spot interview because it revealed the Englishman as a moron. He is not moronic; he is merely embarrassed, outraged that he should be expected to expose himself in public.

The Englishman, then, is reserved: a truism come true. And if one accepts that an East Anglian is an Englishman, only more so — well, you can sympathize with Lord Tollemache's reticence. If your family has been around locally since 1180, if you have a 6,000 acre estate in Suffolk, with a second estate of 5,000 acres at Peckforton Castle in Cheshire, if you have oaks 1,000 years old at the bottom of your garden . . . perhaps the statement has been made and all that remains is to get on with things.

Getting on with things begins early each day for Lord Tollemache. He is at his estate office desk, opening the mail, dictating letters to his secretary, consulting with his agent before motoring to Ipswich four days a week to another office at Cliff Brewery where he is a director. Starting at the brewery, rolling barrels, putting corks in bottles, he has graduated to a desk marginally smaller than Salisbury Plain from where, among other jobs, his responsibilities include a brief on the company's advertising policy. A policy which favoured the William Rushton 'You're lucky, you're in Tolly country' campaign.

Lord Tollemache wears a dark blue pin-striped suit

because he has just come from the funeral of his oldest farm tenant who has died at the age of 94. The river Orwell passes the window; Sheba, his black labrador, is curled into a chair. His brewery secretary brings two cups of tea.

'It's important not just to sit on one's broad acres, taking in the air and the beautiful countryside. The commercial challenge of the brewery is important because it's stretching me in another dimension... yes, it's necessary to be stretched. This way there's always something to do: Helmingham, the brewery, Cheshire, a certain amount of time in London.

'When my father died something had to go, so I chose four days at the brewery to give me more time for the estate. It can be confusing, so that occasionally I have a guilt complex at being in the wrong place at the wrong time. Yes, I enjoy the brewery... but to be honest I'd rather be looking at acres of wheat than at barrels of beer. I believe Helmingham needs me more as well — out of 10 brewery directors, six are directly from the founding family... whereas my ties to the estate and tenants are total. Little things... well, not so little really — we wanted to go away for Christmas one year, which would have meant cutting the traditional Boxing Day shoot. There was such an outcry that we had to change our plans and stay. Half my feeling for Helmingham is responsibility, the other half love; you can't separate the two.

'But the responsibility is nagging. It's always there in my mind... it's been our responsibility for so many hundreds of years that I'd hate my generation to fail the past. This is why we open the gardens in summer, it's why my wife makes jam to sell, why she runs the craft shop, why we sell teas — sadly, the 60p entrance fee doesn't even cover costs, but if we're lucky enough to live here I think it's a pleasure that should be shared. It's also a way of letting people see the problems of keeping the place alive as a family house instead of turning it over to the National Trust or making it into a museum.

'It would be difficult to open the house itself, because it's not a grand palace, the staircases weren't designed to take huge traffic... and I wouldn't be too keen on having people watch me eating lunch. I daren't really pick a lettuce on open days in case visitors see me and think they can pick lettuces as well.

'I'd like to think it will still be much the same in 500 years' time. It would be lovely to think that, but I sometimes think I'm a fool — so many things are stacked against it. Our commitment is total . . . my wife has to run the house, bring up a family in it, entertain in it and run the open days which I think she does brilliantly. But the future . . . supposing my son wanted to go sheep farming in Australia? I'd be disappointed but I couldn't blame him

I was very drawn to Kenya at one time, the white hunter's life seemed ideal, but I matured . . . there was never really a choice as the elder son, I had no option, my life was predetermined, so there was little point in thinking about it. I didn't look too far afield. Also I was moulded into a pattern by a wonderfully united family, so that I was always conscious of my role in an historical context . . . for centuries the family living in the same rooms, looking at the same views.

'In much the same way I consider myself 100% East Anglian. I have the same loyalties to the countryside, to preserving hedgerows, oaks, wildlife, flowers. To the people as well, of course . . . they have this incredibly dry wit and they're immensely kind hearted.'

The drive from the brewery to Helmingham takes 20 minutes, Lord Tollemache at the wheel of a Ford estate car, accelerating from the town quickly. Once at Helmingham he changes from his suit into jeans, jersey, wind-cheater; with the sartorial transformation he assumes another personality, the business executive becoming the countryman. He signs letters dictated to his estate secretary in the morning; matters of leases, agreements, farm buildings are discussed with his agent, John Dickinson. He collects a Jack Russell terrier to join an outing with Sheba: 'The father's called Colonel Black, the grandfather Brigadier Brown, so we thought we'd call this one Private Parts, but he turned out to be a she, so we call her Fanny.' Across the drawbridge next to collect a Range Rover before setting off to take a look at crops, mainly wheat, barley, peas, rape. Over fields, along rutted tracks, the mechanised progress putting up pheasants and partridges, the dogs in the back quivering with excitement.

The Rover pulls up at Jim Cracknell's cottage. Jim is one of the two gamekeepers. Talk is of hatching; in a warm spring wild partridge eggs would be hatched by now, but the cold is putting things back. They take a look at a black labrador Jim is training for Lord Tollemache. 'He'll be a good one, it's in his blood,' says Jim. 'All the same,' replies Lord Tollemache, 'I shan't risk taking him to Scotland this first season.'

The next stop is to see the farm manager, Mr. English, where the talk is of the crops' colour, of the pests likely to attack next and whether it is worth £11 an acre to combat the onslaught, and when the deer culling should begin.

'I didn't know wheat from barley when I started — you learn, you just have to learn. Look at that,' breaking at a turn in the lane where the country unfurls, graceful as a Constable. 'Now that's what I call Suffolk . . . trees and hedgerows and sky. There are too few hedgerows today; I make a rule that hedgerows should be cut back only every 10 years or so. It gives you a sense of enclosure which is particularly Suffolk.

'If there's one single fear I have it's that of revolution. I believe that change is a necessary and a vital part of life, and that it is almost always a good thing, providing it is not too radical or sudden; revolution is one thing — changes in the social structure of society another.

'For example, the first Lord Tollemache was made a peer for his services to agriculture, not just spending his resources on building farm houses for his tenants, and cottages for his labourers, but for being the coiner of the phrase "Three acres and a cow" in Cheshire, and giving likewise an acre to every cottage in Suffolk so that everyone had his own land to grow crops. His idea was in 19th century terms "revolutionary", but it gave immense benefits to his tenants and all those who lived on his estates.

'I've only been "in the saddle" for three years, but I should like to think that my generation can do something equally worthwhile. If Helmingham is to survive, I the landowner must ensure that I adapt to the times, and move ahead of current social changes. I should like to feel that people who live on the Helmingham estate will not just be able to look out of their windows and see more trees and hedgerows and unspoilt Suffolk than anywhere else, but that they will feel that it is really worthwhile to *live* on the estate, and that they are receiving genuine benefits — better farms, better cottages and a more immediate reaction to their problems than if they lived elsewhere.'

One is reminded most forcibly of a sense of survival within the Hall of Helmingham, above which flies the Tollemache fret — or standard. The two drawbridges are raised each night, as they have been since 1510, the Hall thus becoming a moat-enclosed island — which has witnessed history in the making...

Queen Elizabeth I came twice to Helmingham, first in 1561 and later to attend the christening of one of the 10 consecutive generations of Lionel Tollemaches, as her godson. (History repeated itself 400 years later when the Prince of Wales became godfather to the present Lord Tollemache's son, Edward.) As a gift on one of these visits Queen Elizabeth left an orpharion, or lute, made by John Rose in 1580 — the only one in the world. It looks new, as if the gift were made yesterday.

How fresh and legible is the hand of King Charles II in his letters, from exile in Paris, to Elizabeth Tollemache, in gratitude for the use of Helmingham as one of the headquarters of the secret Society of the Sealed Knot, which was instrumental in restoring the monarch to his throne. It was rumoured that the same lady was the Lord Protector's mistress — which speaks volumes for her dedication to the crown, especially when you view Cromwell's portrait, warts and all, at Helmingham.

In every room the likenesses of Tollemaches, long since in their graves, stare down upon the rooms in which once they lived and breathed, flourished and multiplied. King James I is there, so too Charles II; to say nothing of two collaborators who put self-interest before fealty. Lord Tollemache regards the canvas in the sardonic vein of Browning's nobleman surveying Frà Pandolf's painting of his duchess:

'Much the same smile? This grew; I gave commands;
Then all smiles stopped together.'

Chilling lines; yet no less chilling is Lord Tollemache's condemnation of treachery: 'Those two paid the price — they were hung, drawn and quartered. One was dead and buried at the time, so they dug him up to hang, draw and quarter the wretch's body.'

Like the oak trees in the park, the Tollemaches of Helmingham have deep roots in this good Suffolk soil. Here they are and here, one likes to think, they will remain; caring for their home, their lands, the tenants they serve. The politics of envy, which would divest them of responsibility as well as privilege, are the politics of small men. Their argument is easily refuted: if a greengrocer is allowed to bequeath his property to whom he chooses, why should it not be the same for a peer?

'Do you know, there are 80 clocks in this house and they all keep good time. They're not self-winding, someone has to go round doing it, making sure that everything is ticking. I suppose you could say that love keeps things ticking, that love makes Helmingham a living, breathing family home instead of a museum.'

The Media Man: Dick Joice

IN THE WAY of most celebrities, Dick Joice is public property. Whether in Norwich or Needham Market, King's Lynn or Kersey, he is recognised. His is a genial face, avuncular, everyone's friend. The sort of face you can trust; matching well with a manner suggesting the solid East Anglian virtue of wryness — a bit slow, perhaps, disinclined to be hurried. He is Everyman's East Anglian, determined to do things in his own way and in his own good time. Television discovered in him the typical, turning him, by constant exposure, into the archetypal. When complete strangers come up to him in the street, addressing him as 'Dick', it is because they see in him something of themselves.

Mind you, it wasn't always the case: 'The family, we think, came from Ireland about 300 years ago and were either cattle dealers or stealers, and I reckon they walked a lot of bullocks from Ireland as far as they could get and settled in East Norfolk. Perhaps one of them couldn't spell, put an "i" instead of a "y", and Joyce became Joice. My grandfather was a farm foreman, eventually became a farmer but died with nothing.

'My father, born in 1888, seeing what conditions were like on the land, shot off to Canada when they offered a square mile of land if you cleared it. He took one look at it, decided it wasn't for him, worked his passage back and walked home from Liverpool. He became a smallholder, then took a farm before the First World War, married my mother, couldn't go into the forces because of a congenital heart condition which he apparently passed on to us. By the beginning of the depression he was farming 5,000 acres, all rented; the interesting thing is that some of the land, now worth £1,000 or more an acre, he rented at a penny an acre a year — just shows how land was going out of production in the 1920's and 30's. The way he kept his head above water was because he was very far-seeing: he saw that machinery was here to stay, so he gradually got rid of his horses and became mechanised; he also moved labour about, he bought a lot of old charabancs and instead of having static labour on the farms — he had 13 farms — he moved the men about. He was a tenant of Lord Townshend, Lord Leicester and Sir Thomas Cook, but he never owned land until quite late in life, and then not very much.

'My own first memories are of living in the very small house at Great Ryburgh, near Fakenham, where father rented 250 acres, his first real farm. I remember practical things, like being with father when he was building chicken huts, watching my mother skinning rabbits, going with father in the pony cart to Fakenham. They were obviously living on a shoestring because I remember the detail of small amounts, like selling eggs and butter — it helped with cash between harvests to pay the wages.

'I suppose we were on the bottom end of the yeoman farmer scale... my father told me once that he inadvertently heard himself discussed between two big farmers: "Oh," said one, "it's some little chap who's just beginning, and I don't give much for his chances — his name's Charles Joice". The only other thing I remember about those times of depression, apart from the general atmosphere of austerity in which things had to be used and used and used again, was one Christmas going into Jarrold's store in Norwich and asking my mother if Father Christmas couldn't give me a small mechanical toy, and being told no. I created over this — so much so that my mother burst into tears, and I remember to this day mother standing in Jarrold's toy department in her little potty hat, crying because she couldn't afford what I wanted for Christmas, and I remember my father taking me to task over it when we got home.'

Poverty is always a matter of perspective: the man with a Mini is poorer than the man with a Rover; the barefoot boy is poorer than the boy with shoes. The Joice family may not have been rich, but neither were they poor and later on they were able to send Dick to a private school, Culford. It was here, during his last year at school in 1936, that he first came into contact with television: 'The physics master and two of us boys built a Baird television, and furthermore we got an image in Bury St. Edmunds from London. I didn't have a set myself for the last Coronation, but soon after that Lord Townshend — I was a tenant on his estate — came to see me and said: "They've asked me to front up the consortium to put in for the Independent Television Authority's licence for this area." I laughed and said, "Well, you're just the chap, you haven't got a television set either." He asked me would I be interested — I said yes, I was interested in anything.

'It happened, you see, that I'd started, with a friend, Norfolk Mobile Cinemas — we went around to the village halls with a pair of projectors showing what you could see in the towns: a big picture, the news, and a short. But if the seating was under 200 in any of the halls there was no entertainment tax, so you could do it for a shilling — and we did very well. Incidentally, television killed that stone dead, so it was a good job I was in television by then. I'd also made one or two very amateurish farming films... well, anyway, Lord Townshend and the other directors asked me if I'd help set up the farming office.

'Eventually they gave me a screen test — I've never been very serious and I certainly wasn't about that, but they seemed to think that because my head was fairly fat — it was the right aspect ratio — it would fit the screen. So they offered me the job of presenting *Farming Diary*. I told them that they would have to take me as I was, that with half a million pounds worth of technical equipment I refused to go round it — it must go round me. What I meant was that I refused to be anything else but myself.

'Anyway, they still spent weeks rehearsing me and on the 27th October 1959, on the first night final rehearsal, I knew exactly what I had to say: "Good evening, my name is Dick Joice. I'm a farmer from East Raynham...", but what it came out as was, "Good evening, my name is East Raynham — I live at Dick Joice." ' Since it was rather late to employ a stand-in, he was quietly instructed to forget his lines, relax and simply *chat* to the camera — to be himself. It is what he did then, what he has been doing ever since, in programmes such as *About Anglia, Bygones,* and countless feature films. He has made a career, or at least a second career, out of being himself.

'Yes, of course I have to agree that television breeds materialism among us — we hanker after better cars; our children hanker after too many sweets... but what I fear most is the violence on the screen. But what do you do?

You can't not invent the thing; perhaps it would be better if it hadn't been invented. Does it shape or misshape us? I don't think I can give a direct answer to that — but if I had to I'd say misshape. My own contribution hardly comes into this category because my stuff isn't controversial . . . as a director of Anglia I've always taken the line that television has moved too fast, but I'm only one voice. If I had my way I'd impose a censor.'

For a farmer from East Raynham there was room at the top, and Dick Joice scaled the heights. In comparable feats of social mountaineering, contestants usually collect a few scars. The fact that Dick Joice's 24 years old marriage ended in divorce; the fact that, after a period of black-outs, he underwent open-heart surgery, may or may not be connected to a television lifestyle. Even rose-growers get divorced and suffer heart conditions. Ask Dick Joice whether he has ever regretted his involvement with television, he replies: 'There is one very small part of regret; had I realised what becoming public property by appearing in everyone's home would mean, I may not have done it. You know, someone comes up to me in Sudbury or wherever and says, "Hullo, Dick, you opened our fête 17 years ago" . . . and I'm meant to remember it! It's annoying, this loss of privacy. I will admit that in the early days my ego was boosted — I'll never forget the first time it hit me: I was walking around Castle Meadow in Norwich when Sir Edmund Bacon, the Lord Lieutenant for Norfolk, came up to me. He's a pretty important man and he always seems about nine feet high. "Ah, young Dick," he said, "wanted to run into you. You're a damned nuisance — every evening between five past six and seven o'clock I have to watch that wretched thing because I just can't miss what you *might* say and it wastes too much of my time." It never occurred to me that those sort of people watched, although perhaps it should have.

'Yes, I've got to agree that television has spelt the end of family entertainment. I remember the days when we hadn't got a wireless and my father said, "I'm not having one of those things, it'll upset all our lives." We sat with our oil lamps — we hadn't got electricity then — and when the wireless finally came into the house in 1936, father would only have it on for the news and very special programmes. So the family, my older brother and younger sister, made our own entertainment — and we were in bed by nine, parents by 10. And we were busy; we were all given jobs on the farm, helping in the dairy, washing eggs, feeding and plucking poultry, there wasn't much time left over.'

Of his Norfolk heritage: 'I do think East Anglia feels it is nice and comfortably insulated; and if anyone wanted to slip off to do something else, he went anyway. I think there's a basic practical honesty you won't find in the centre of industrial cities ... there's this confrontation with nature — you know you can't do anything to speed up the harvest, but surely it will come. It's helped me in all sorts of ways when I've said to myself, "I can't do anything about that, but it'll happen anyway". It's said of me that I'm a patient man, and I think it's because I have a knack of judging when it pays to wait. I think we have a basically honest way of looking at it all — perhaps we're just naive — or out of touch.

'Out of touch with some things, but very much in touch with the land — it's something you have a *feeling* about, you can't put a name to it or a label on it. I'm much happier on the land. Television makes the adrenalin flow, it's a great experience — but it mustn't last too long. It's very immediate, things change by the hour, by the second when you're on — but in fact I'd say it was much the same after a while as the bloke in a factory putting the same nut on a car on a conveyor belt. It gets to the point when if the tea wagon is two minutes late, they want to shoot the lady bringing it. But farming goes on, gently changing all the time — you can't be a clock watcher.

'In television you've got to be damn careful to use your sense of responsibility because you're not playing to a big audience, but to a small room of two or three people who can't turn you off until they've decided they don't like what you've said — by which time you've given offence. I've never *ever* given any indication what my politics are for this reason. I try to behave as if I'm an actual guest in their sitting room, and you wouldn't be rude then, would you?'

In this part of Norfolk, Nelson is the hero; the admiral is remembered as few men have ever been. Dick Joice has a second hero, Jimmy Coe, a farm worker long since dead. It was in the early days of militant trade unionism: 'Somehow those old boys, Jimmy Coe in particular, although they appeared extreme and left wing, really worked for the good of the community; and they helped to bring farmworkers up to their present conditions. They were sensible people. They had to take an extreme view in order to be heard, but when it came to the crunch they were practical.

'My father had a strike on his hands just prior to harvest; he couldn't come to terms with the men because he hadn't the money to offer any more. They went on strike . . . well, old Jimmy Coe came over on his bicycle from Castle Acre, about 12 miles, and he talked to the men and then he talked to my father. He weighed up everything like an old judge before he went back to the men — and I remember exactly what he told them. 'Dew yew go back tew work," he said, "Dew yew try an' git ivery thin' yew want an' yew'll ind up wi nawthin'." '

* * * * * *

Dick Joice and his second wife, Jean, live on a smallholding in a pair of farm cottages they converted. They keep a Jersey cow for milk, and a few Jacob sheep. They are almost self-supporting, making their own bread, cheese, butter. In their sitting room is a video-recorder so that Dick can play back Anglia programmes in order to comment to the Anglia management. From their windows you cannot see another house, just Norfolk commonland.

At the back of the house they designed and built an extension, their library-study — a lot of the work they did themselves. The outside walls are traditional Norfolk flint, each flint gathered from nearby fields. It was a backbreaking task. Give or take a few, they picked up 11,000 flints.

The Shopkeeper: George Bumstead

SOUTHWOLD is an invincibly respectable place, a retirement colony on sea, yet also close to Suffolk farming traditions: it feels the pull of both sea and land. Which is the only contrary aspect of its nature.

Stradbroke Road is a terrace of Victorian villas. George Bumstead's name is above the door of number five because he is a general grocer. His shop has nothing to do with supermarketry; it has a solid mahogany counter, a hand-operated bacon slicer, farmhouse chairs for customers to take the weight off their feet. It sells everything from Vim to exotic cheeses, home-cooked hams to Turkish delight. There are two assistants who nowadays call people 'dear'. This bewilders Mr. Bumstead: 'We were always a "sir" and "madam" shop before. An elderly spinster customer told me recently that she'd never been called dear in her life, and I thought that sounded rather lonely.'

Mr. Bumstead's father established a grocery business in the High Street in 1911, but died young so that George was conscripted into the trade part-time when he was 13 and full-time when he left Southwold School at 14. In 1940 he was called up, serving as an RAF fitter-armourer until 1946 when he opened Bumstead's in Stradbroke Road.

Meanwhile, in 1939 at St. Edmund's Church, he had married Phyllis, daughter of a Southwold fishing family. They met at school. For honeymoon they set off by car, but 'there was petrol rationing and our coupons ran out at Bedford — so we stayed there, at the Bridge Hotel'. They have a son, Bill, a civil engineer; and a daughter, Hilary, living in London as a speech therapist. Mr. and Mrs. Bumstead live above the shop with their dog, Oy. They have no garden.

'Local people?' George Bumstead reflects. 'Well, there's a story our retired vicar, the Reverend Theodore Child, tells against himself: he met his wife at Southampton

University and she thought he was rather peculiar, but eventually married him — and when she came to live in East Anglia she discovered that all other East Anglians were exactly the same. It's all changed now, of course, people who have come to retire in Southwold are from a different background, they're largely retired professional people or from big business . . . in the old days our local aristocracy were largely people who had never worked — they were privileged. I suppose this all stems from the social revolution which started in 1945, I should say. I see myself as a classless person. The county people don't talk down to me and the milkman doesn't talk up to me.

'The local Southwold man is almost becoming extinct — when a local dies, his house is usually bought by someone from another area. We're almost being taken over. They buy what they think of as a quaint fisherman's cottage, and spend as much again on pulling the place to pieces to turn into a sort of fisherman's penthouse. Young locals can't afford these prices, so they move out into council estates in places like Reydon . . . to work in the building trade, some even to London. Tradesmen have come down in the social scale. When I was a boy the butcher or the baker was someone, he might be the mayor and people thought highly of him, he had more money, he was able to give credit . . . today he's dropped a few rungs on the ladder.'

A treacherous sea scours these shores — shallower than most, saltier, vicious. It is the anvil upon which character has been forged: 'Visitors think of Southwold as a fun town, but there is a harsh, almost brutal touch . . . if you were here when we had our most recent argument with the sea, you'd come to realise what a tough existence it can be. You'd also realise that there's something man can do absolutely nothing about. If the sea . . . mother nature, the Good Lord, decides to drive the sea in over the top of us, there's nothing we could do. It gives you a feeling of respect. I'm not quite sure what I mean by this, but we've got a nuclear power station nearby at Sizewell, and we've got American airfields loaded with atomic devices . . . but the sea is really unstoppable.

'When this town survived entirely from fishing, when a man kept his family by what he took from the sea . . . and if that man drowned, there'd be no pension, no compensation . . . the women were in constant fear of widowhood and poverty. I still feel conscious of how near we are to nature and disaster. Bad weather still makes us anxious, especially wind — I think this town is unnerved by high wind because we know lives are at stake. I mean, last week they fished three men out of the sea . . . not local, from a Greek ship off Lowestoft. Holiday makers never treat this sea with the respect it deserves. There's a bathing death nearly every year . . . it's not just sunbathing, picnics and paddling, this sea is deadly too.

'I think men of the sea and men of the land here are very special breeds, alike in some ways but opposites in others. Farmers cultivate and give back to the land. The fisherman just takes . . . they're the hunters: they say the sea is running out of fish. But I think I admire men of the sea more . . . for instance my father-in-law still has a boat at 87; it's been taken from under him two or three times, but he's had it repaired. He stopped fishing for a living last year but he can't keep away — used to follow the herring shoals as his father did and his father before that. He's tough, determined, stubborn if you like, not very sociable; they looked after their families, their old folk in particular. I have very strong feelings about people looking after their old and not putting them away in homes. These kinds of men are self-supporting, the Welfare State, hand-outs, mean nothing to them. They despise charity. They have this feeling for the sea . . . they can read the signs, the tides, the moon comes into it a lot — I really don't think the Met. Office think much about the moon — but fishermen put a lot in store by it. Instinct too . . . my father-in-law would know where the fish were. It was bred in his bones.

'They're God fearing too. They may not go to church, but they fear God all right. Most people who face danger do — perhaps it's an insurance, but they believe too that the elements are controlled by someone outside it all. That's not to say they're not superstitious as well. We had a family called Smith, always put to sea wearing bowler hats because "you couldn't capsize if you wore a bowler".'

It would be hard to describe the Bumsteads as highlivers: occasionally they go to friends for a drink or a meal, but never reciprocate hospitality. 'I'm surprised we're still invited out. We don't entertain because I think it's a bit primitive living over the shop, a bit shabby. We never really had a house, just a workhouse. But we love it when the children bring their friends. They wear jeans and long hair and they're too liberated to care that the settee springs are coming through. They seem to feel for things — the environment, pollution, health foods. Yes, I like that.

'I don't really think I'm a pleasure man; more a cart-horse than a racehorse. I think I was built for work more than play. I have a reputation for being a bit of a misery — I don't smile easily. A parson once told someone I'd be more cheerful if I did things for other people. Funny really, perhaps he didn't know about my voluntary work . . .'

Apart from being Chairman of the St. Raphael Handicapped Club, Chairman of the Friends of Southwold Hospital, Secretary of the Southwold Trust, Mr. Bumstead serves on four other voluntary organisations, taking up three evenings a week. Mrs. Bumstead is booking secretary of the church hall. For 20 years he has worked for the local drama group, as electrician, stage manager, 'general dogsbody'. He has acted as well, his favourite part being Father Schiller in *A Letter from the General.* Today he runs a song-and-dance routine, the Swinging Grandfathers, whose average age is 66. They give shows to audiences like the Southwold Women's Institute.

He recalls being deeply moved once by *Murder in the Cathedral:* 'The chorus, Women of Canterbury I think they were called, chanted something like "living and partly living". It hit me because I feel alive, but not really living. I suppose it's my own choosing. I'm my own man, and if I'm at all sad I've only myself to blame.

'I'm glad I'm the last of the line. The children are well out of it. There's no future in being a family grocer. I wish I could get out before we're wiped out. Taxation today is holding everything back. A man can work longer hours, but take home less money. It's as if there's a plot against the self employed man. Take your car worker; he doesn't risk anything — I risk everything I have. The people who work for me do better than I do. The only thing I have is the premises — they must have increased a lot in value.'

His attitude towards personal freedom is ambivalent: 'We're imprisoned by legislation: there are inspectors for this, that and the other. It's as if we're not trusted. Perhaps it's my job; perhaps a roadmender feels free. I think freedom and law and order are separate . . . if freedom means the right to slash train seats, to break up telephone booths, then I don't want freedom. The 10 commandments give you freedom and discipline — but the gross national product has taken the place of the ten commandments.'

His attitudes towards his home and his job are less convoluted: 'I love the marshes here, the beaches and the dunes at the south end of the town. I love its wildness . . . I prefer it all in winter when the visitors have gone. I know we need them — without the tourists Southwold would die.

'No, I don't really like my job. The only thing that keeps me going is the involvement with customers. I'd really like to have produced something — not on a conveyor belt. I often wonder if a bricklayer ever looks at a wall he's built and thinks to himself "I'm proud of that". There's nothing very aesthetic in selling tins of beans, is there?'

The Factory Worker: Stanley Howes

'NUMBER 36, Thompson Avenue,' says Stanley Howes, giving directions how to find him, 'you know, like the poet.' Most of the roads hereabouts are named after poets: Shakespeare Drive, Shelley Gardens, Wordsworth Crescent. It is a trim housing estate in Lexden, a Colchester suburb. The streets are tree-lined, with grass verges; you can see that householders spend a lot of time in their gardens — each one would do as an advertisement for a seed catalogue.

Number 36 is no exception; the front garden is only a few yards square, but packed with early summer flowers, roses coming into bloom. Such fecundity seems almost to dwarf the red brick bungalow. Stanley Howes is pottering among his shrubs; he enjoys 'pottering', he says, nothing serious, but he likes to see things nice. Susie, their Dalmatian, barks hysterically, leaping up at the wrought-iron gate, a three year old plum-pudding bitch.

'She's all right,' Stanley reassures, 'we spoil her, I'm afraid. She doesn't bite.' In fact, she is rather sloppy, nuzzling into your palm, soft-eyed, as Stanley leads the way into the sitting room. He is a well-preserved 58, a man who takes care of his appearance; his fair-greying hair is brushed, hands scrupulously clean. He wears a fawn light-weight suit, polo-neck jersey, leather sandals over blue socks. Pale eye-lashes give him the vulnerable look of a nocturnal creature — perhaps a part-time nocturnal creature.

'Two weeks I work days, then two weeks nights,' he explains. 'At Woods of Colchester — it was a private company, but now we're part of G.E.C. We manufacture industrial and domestic fans . . . a work force of about 1,700. I'm a mechanical inspector, I inspect small components. Yes, I'm a shop steward — it's the Amalgamated Union of Engineering Workers, but I'm not very militant . . . I must say there are a few militant ones about. My views make me a bit unpopular — I'm not so bad now, calming down, I suppose, but the unions are getting too strong, too much power. Frankly, I can't see where it's going to end — it's encouraging laziness, people thinking money grows on trees. And apathetic managements have succumbed because they're out of touch.

'The older ones, ones who've had it rough, they don't scrounge or skive. It's the younger ones; I notice when men aren't working, they talk and laze, there's no sense of urgency — but what can you do? They know they can't be sacked. More or less the only things you can be sacked for are theft and violence, they're the only reasons that I can recall. There's not many who want to work today, and that's why we're in a muddle — we *are* in a muddle, aren't we? As a shop steward I try to sort out problems with management — not that we have many at Woods, they're good employers; and I'm a signatory to pay agreements — I've yet to hear of anyone turning down a pay rise!'

He selects a pipe from a rack, feeds Three Nuns tobacco into the bowl and strikes the first of many Swan Vestas. The bungalow has two bedrooms, kitchen and bathroom, and the room we are in — a room in which there is not one picture, not one photograph, no books. There is stereo music equipment, a china tea service displayed in a glass cabinet, a tape recorder. Stanley is on the sofa, puffing at his pipe, looking at his feet, at the mantelpiece clock; he finds it hard to meet your eyes and, when he does, glances away quickly. His evasion is a shy gesture, an unsureness.

'Probably I'm as I am because of my background, that's it — father came to Essex from the north country because he couldn't find work there, so I was brought up with the fear of unemployment, and gratitude when you were working. I went to Mile End Council School in Colchester, then on to Technical College. At 16 I left to be a mechanic at Willet's garage, they were Ford dealers — war came then and I volunteered for the Royal Army Service Corps. It was a busy war. I was at Dunkirk, went to Durban in South Africa on the troopship *Arawa* . . . . I'll always remember that old tub, we were scared because of enemy submarines — they shut us below decks when subs were about and we didn't think much of that. The Middle East next, the 8th Army desert campaign under Monty — Alamein, then through to Italy and Sicily. Afterwards I stayed on another couple of years in Vienna, driving Displaced Persons, and got demobbed in '47. Joined Paxman's in Colchester then — stayed there until I was 38 when I was made redundant. That was nasty. Out of work six months until Woods took me on. I've got a lot to thank the company for.'

Stanley's wife, Joyce, is also at Woods, in the office. Her family was bombed out in London during the blitz, when she was evacuated to Colchester. She joined Woods in 1942. She became a Sunday School teacher at St. Peter's, where she and Stanley were married.

Susie, haunches down on the carpet, still as a porcelain book-end, begins to whine. Stanley pats her soothingly: 'All right, all right, Joyce will be home soon,' he says. 'It's a good marriage. The wife and I have just grown into each other somehow — it's been a long time.' His eyes wander again, confused. 'Men don't analyse these things — women do maybe. I'm just incomplete without her . . . I'm not putting that very well, but it's what I feel. That's the worst thing about night shift, I miss being with her. She'll be home for tea soon.

'Getting back to work . . . . .' He re-lights his pipe, anxious to return to firmer ground. 'There doesn't seem to be enough communication between workers and management. We never really see the governors, someone just takes a quick walk through the factory once a week. I'd like to see the directors among the workers, talking to us. It's like we ask ourselves "Who am I working for — Mr. Weinstock in Birmingham?" . . . . he's the G.E.C. supremo. I don't think workers feel part of anything, more like numbers.

'No, I don't wish I'd gone on the land. No doubt there's the same attitude there, among the young. It's the value of money that's not appreciated generally. I went into engineering because I wrote an essay at school and it won a prize . . . you'd think that if you were looking at motors all your life you'd get fed up, but there's something different in every machine. Any job can get boring — I expect you can have bored millionaires.

'I'll retire in seven years. I'm not looking forward to it. Wouldn't mind a little cottage with a bit of garden, but they're so expensive. We paid £2,500 for this house 16 years ago — it's worth 11 or £12,000 now. I don't care about dying. I had this ulcer a while ago — it blew up. It was worry, I suppose. The company was very good to me, and when I came back the canteen did a special diet . . . I was spared . . . I think I've had a good life. It's bound up with religion. I'm not religious, but I'm not irreligious, if you see what I mean.

'We don't know many of the neighbours; you don't pop into people's houses as they do up north. They all do it there and no one minds. It's more a "good-day" relationship here. It's a quiet area. We might go across to the Truscott's for a Sunday morning drink, and they might come here . . . they've got a Hammond organ, and Joyce and I are fond of music. Classical music, I'm not a lover of pop. Mozart is my favourite composer. We go to concerts at St. Botolph's church, and to the Gilbert and Sullivan operas the dramatic society put on. And we like going to the seaside, Clacton when we had a car, but I don't fancy the roads today with all that traffic — I had a bit of nervous trouble with the ulcer. . . . I've got a Yamaha motor bike now to get to work on. We've been to Majorca six times. It's nice there, it's the climate — but we don't really do much.

'Regrets? I think we regret not having children. I don't know why we didn't. We never really went into it — didn't see doctors and things. We didn't like to talk about it. We talk about it now, but I don't think we're bitter. We've learnt to be reliant on each other, you see. Perhaps we feel a bit lonely sometimes . . . if one of us dies before the other . . . that's something I don't dwell on.'

His pipe has gone out again, but he seems not to notice. He glances about the room, looking for substance, his attention falling on Susie. Do you want to go out, he asks her. 'They're usually highly-strung, Dalmatians,' he says informatively. 'But Susie's not bad really; she's very devoted. You wouldn't like a glass of sherry?' Suddenly, he is conscious of his role as host. No, he doesn't mind talking; he doesn't mind helping: 'I've always been a sympathetic listener too,' he says. 'There's not much kindness about . . . . even so it *has* been a good life. These displaced people I drove around at the end of the war — they'd seen such misery, I think it opened my eyes. Sometimes they make me think of this country and what's happening — we used to be a great nation. Something's got to happen. We're not quite like the Spanish or the Italians, but people are beginning to shrug their shoulders and say, "Why bother". Governments, I don't care whether Labour or Conservative, they don't give me much confidence. We don't seem to throw up good leaders these days.'

He moves into the garden to say goodbye. There is a humility about him, a deference; you can see that he is not a militant trade unionist. 'This magnolia,' he touches its leaves. 'I bought two of them from Woolworths 20 years ago for half a crown. You should see it in spring. The other one died . . . they're very tender when they're young.' He seems about to say more, but changes his mind, unlatching the gate. 'Thank you for coming,' he says, avoiding your eyes. 'It's been very interesting.'

He calls Susie back off the pavement. He closes the gate, waving briefly before turning to look the length of Thompson Avenue, waiting to see if Joyce is coming home for tea.

The Meals-on-Wheels helper: Jeanie Marcel

THE RADIO told us that Friday had been the coldest night for 10 years. Frost appeared as an exquisite decoration; children made slides along the ice, and those whose knew how skated on village ponds. Water pipes froze; there was a boom in the sale of paraffin. Then the snows came, and with it hazard warnings on motorways. Icicles hung from gutters like stilettos and somewhere an old lady, living alone, was stabbed by the winter ferocity. They called it hypothermia — which means she froze to death.

Three or four days later a yellow Renault 4 burrows through the starched white lanes of West Suffolk, from Stanningfield to Bury St. Edmunds. At the wheel is Jeanie Marcel, on her way to W.V.S. Meals-on-Wheels duty. Her husband is managing director of a local firm of agricultural engineers; they have two grown up daughters, and live in a circa 1700 farmhouse. John Marcel has a gun in a local syndicate, giving him a day's shooting most weeks. They holiday regularly in France; Jeanie's mother, in her early 70's, has just returned from a trip to Barbados. The Marcels are in 'fortunate' circumstances.

'I found that I wasn't really doing anything for anyone else, so I took up Meals-on-Wheels. It's doing a service for people who deserve something. I think everyone who is able should try to help people who are unconnected with their usual life. This is called the Hawstead Round, about 29 miles from start to finish, calling on 16 people. I do it once a month, but the round is operated three times a week, each time providing someone with a hot dinner — main course and pudding — for 20p.'

In Bury Jeanie Marcel heads for St. Mary's Hospital, the old hospital, parking her car outside the kitchen. It is 11 am and Les James, the chef, is almost ready to serve the day's menu: roast beef and Yorkshire pudding with roast and mashed potatoes, swedes and gravy; then chocolate pudding with custard. Generous helpings are served into individual metal containers which are transferred in bulk to an insulated hamper and loaded into the car.

The first call is at Horringer-cum-Ickworth, just beyond the great iron gates of Ickworth Park — 1,800 acres of it, 11 miles round — home of the Hervey family, Earls and Marquesses of Bristol. The house in its present style was begun c.1794 by Fredk. Earl of Bristol and Bishop of Derry. It is a brick building, stuccoed, on a front of over 200 yards. There is a domed rotunda, seemingly large enough to contain an entire council housing estate, modelled by Francis Sandys from the plans of the Roman architect Asprucci. There are state rooms, a distinguished picture collection, a walled garden with a red-brick greenhouse dating from 1714 when Vanbrugh visited the Herveys. The present Lord Bristol's shooting parties offer sport to royalty and the internationally celebrated.

Mrs. Steers has gnomes along her garden path, and she has spread an immaculate table napkin, set with a spoon, for her dinner. But she won't eat it now, she says, she'll save it for a bit, pop it in her oven to keep warm. She may save the chocolate pudding for this evening, or perhaps tomorrow. The heat from the oven keeps the cottage warm; and Mrs. Steers has visitors, so she has not been marooned by the social tides of Horringer. She is deaf, watching your lips anxiously as you talk. She manages to understand that which is necessary, replying that she will be glad when the thaw comes. 'Thank you ever so much for coming,' she says, and motions towards the two 10p coins on the table as if she is embarrassed to mention money. She plucks at her pinafore, opening the door. Be careful on them roads, she warns, caring for our safety.

Just along this neatly manicured village green lives Mrs. Nutter. We let ourselves in at the front door before which, on a little table, is a post-card printed in pencil capitals: 'THANK YOU FOR COMING. COME AGAIN FRIDAY PLEASE.' The cottage is silent. 'Good morning, Mrs. Nutter,' calls Jeanie Marcel, 'are you all right?' From another room a muffled voice says, 'Good morning... yes, thank you.' Silence again. In five years Jeanie has seen Mrs. Nutter once. 'She keeps very much to herself.' But everything is clean and tidy, and there is no apparent cause for worry. Anyway, you can smell when things are wrong; tragedy has an odour all of its own.

Mrs. Clark's estate, across the road, has been reduced to one small room; her bed is in the corner. But it is cosy, and on her well-blacked stove she is cooking for a friend. There are family photos, a lot of photos, and a budgie in a cage she calls Jacky. 'Someone gave him to me. I thought he'd talk . . . be a bit of company, then this friend bought him that mirror. Now he just sits looking at himself and doesn't say nothing.' Mrs. Clark thanks us for coming. As we leave, she is staring into her grate, while Jacky stares chirpily at his own reflection — the old lady with Narcissus, her budgie.

Mr. Sargent comes next, a real ladies' man, spruced up in a well-creased suit, faultlessly shaved for the occasion of his meal on a wheel. He started work on the Bristol estate in 1913 for 3s. 6d. a week, 6 am until 6 pm; then he went into the house to polish and scrub and hump logs for the fires. 'They almost bent me double, the weight of those logs . . . I had 25 years then looking after St. Leonard's churchyard, and now I've been retired 14 years. Love it! Miss my wife, though. They say that time heals, but they don't know the truth of it. My dear wife said before she went that she'd never worry about me . . . she'd taught me to cook, you see.' Mr. Sargent says he has a girl friend, but they're just good friends, nothing serious. 'You see, I miss my dear wife too much.'

Mr. Catchpole, a way out of the village, has one room and a kitchen; the lavatory is at the end of the garden. He is sitting by a scarcely flickering kitchen fire, nursing a cup of tea his visiting sister has brewed. He is shivering violently and does not appear to understand why we have come. He stares uncomprehendingly as Jeanie serves his roast beef. His speech is inarticulate and he smiles mirthlessly, as if savouring some decayed joke against himself. His clothes need obvious attention. The other room has just been cleaned by the home help; bed made, a single bar electric fire — the flex of which is coiled like a cobra about to strike — barely keeps the chill at bay. Above Mr. Sargent's bed hang two framed photographs: one is of him as a lad with thick unruly hair, with spirit in his eyes; in the other the eyes are dulled, the hair shorn to the requirements of the uniform of King and Country. He wears drab khaki, puttees, boots polished to the sheen of a mint sovereign; he has the look of a man old before he was ever young. Mr. Catchpole is 87, an incontinent old soldier.

'He keeps hiding things,' says the home help. 'He lets his fire out and he forgets to eat. He broke his wireless and he hid that electric fire in the food cupboard ... one day he'll get a shock off that fire. He can't help it, poor old fellow. He doesn't mean to be a nuisance — it's just that his mind is going. But they can't move him because there's nothing really wrong with him. That's what the doctor says: there's nothing really wrong with him. If I didn't keep looking in, he wouldn't touch his food and his fire would go out ... then what would happen?'

The two Grimwood brothers come next. They have worked the Whepstead land and lived in the same cottage for 61 years. Long since retired, they are somehow rooted to this spot; it is as if their life blood is in the soil, their sweat too, as well as their hopes and dismays. There is an interdependence between the land and the men who work it, each one committed to the other in a way which is rare in other industries ... committed to or fettered by, it is sometimes hard to tell the difference. Certainly the rewards have been small in terms of the material. Yet they have seen things denied to others of us, learned things we will never know — and this bring a contentment and an order to their lives: *To everything there is a season, and a time to every purpose under the heaven. A time to plant, and a time to pluck up that which is planted.*

The windows of their cottage look across the fields they sowed and harvested; and whoever holds the deeds of title, this land is surely theirs for ever more.

Through inclination they were never great travellers, and today they cannot afford the fare to Bury. 'It's ten and sixpence on the bus — the pension doesn't stretch far these days.' They sit, listening to the wireless, alarmed at the price of anthracite, waiting for another spring to warm the soil and aging bones.

The ceilings are low in Mr. and Mrs. Wilkins' cottage, and the sitting room is dark. Not that it matters much because Mr. Wilkins is going blind. 'I can see your shape,' he says, 'and I can see my wife's red jersey, but I can't see much else, not television. My wife's 90, 12 years older than me. She helps me get around the house ... we help each other.'

They sit either side of the fire; its warmth is the centre

of their universe. Mrs. Wilkins says nothing, simply nods, her head turning from side to side in concentration, reaching for words she is not quite able to find. Mr. Wilkins comes to the door with us, his hands feeling the sharp edges of the table. He is very cheerful. 'It's bright out here,' he says, standing upright, a tall man, in his garden. 'It's the snow — the thaw will come soon. Goodbye and thank you for coming.' He waves, then fumbles with the latch, going inside to rejoin Mrs. Wilkins, so that they can help each other, two against the world.

At Welnetham Mr. and Mrs. Brewer have a bright council house, neat as a new pin. Mr. Brewer has a cough and sits hugging the fire. At 15 he lied about his age so that he could get into the Machine Gun Corps in the Great War. Then came 21 years in the Suffolk Regiment before he came out to work the land. Mrs. Brewer is a bustling, busy person, well able to cope. Nothing, it seems, would daunt her.

On a pleasant nearby estate, in a house called Oasis, next door to High Noon, it is Mr. Vincent who is doing the coping. His wife had a stroke, so he does the fetching and carrying; but he is young in his 70's — he can manage.

So too, in the same street, can Mrs. Norwell, who had a stroke as well. She cannot get to the shops, but she has help; and these are comfortable houses, centrally heated, three bedrooms, large, bright sitting rooms. All mod. cons., you could say, with Meals-on-Wheels as a little extra, as if to show that no one today has been forgotten, that no one is neglected by a Welfare State.

And yet, in an isolated spot near a village we shall call Dapplesford, two men survive a kind of squalor one would not expect in this year of grace and gracious living. 'Squalor' is a strong word...

...but perhaps not strong enough for the style in which Tom Woods and his son Peter face each day. Tom, in his 80's, was a builder; he owns the cottage. His son of 40 is an imbecile, harmless, toothless; he is picking at his hair, examining the findings, crooning in a low animal key. He wears no trousers. Old Tom has a sack over his head to keep out the cold. Both father and son are dirty; the dirt is deep into their pores.

By the broken gate are three milk bottles; the milk has frozen and burst the glass. A further three lie outside the open front door: six wasted pintas. The garden is neglected, a wilderness in which a caravan is parked. The caravan is there, a present, since it was discovered that rats climbed over Mr. Woods and Peter as they lay in bed; it was felt that they would be safe in the caravan. They have not used it once.

The cottage roof is part thatch, part corrugated tin, wholly ineffective at keeping out the weather. There is no running water, sanitation, or electricity; just an oil lamp. Tom Woods and Peter crouch by a fire in the room they live in. They share the room with a detritus of old newspapers, bottles, tins of half devoured food furred with the mould of bacteria. Half eaten food lies on the floor.

How father and son communicate with each other, God alone must know; perhaps flesh and blood have a special language. Jeanie mentions that they could go into care during this bitter spell if they so wish; but Tom isn't having any: 'They can't make me, can they? This is me own house . . . could you stop by the shop and get us some fags, and drinking chocolate and pastry?'

Tom's truculence evaporates as he realises that this is no deputation to move him from his home. There is no self-pity in him. He knows what he wants, which, presumably, is freedom; and Peter knows nothing at all, and that can't harm him. He smiles the awful smile of the insane, teased by gibberish humour. As Jeanie puts out his dinner, offering him the plate, Peter cowers into a dark corner of the room, an animal retreating to his lair. But as we leave, he scrambles forward to wolf up the food with his hands.

Sometime, and it cannot be so very far away, old Tom Woods will find his ultimate freedom; and then, one asks oneself, what will become of Peter and to the seasons of his existence, for *To every thing there is a season, and a time to every purpose under the heaven: a time to be born, and a time to die . . .*

The Commuter: Francis Dodgson

ON 7th MARCH 1975 the Stour Valley village of East Bergholt awoke to find itself caught in a crossfire of publicity. 'Wave of a Brolly Halts Train,' shrieked banner headlines in the *Daily Mirror*. 'Fed-up Francis Hijacks Train with his Brolly,' exclaimed the *Sun*. 'The Artful Dodger gets a roasting from commuters,' bawled the *Evening News*. 'Taking a train by the horns' — *The Guardian*. 'The Dodger stops 7.40 in its tracks,' *Daily Mail*. 'Express Relief for Stopper Dodgson,' *Essex County Standard*. The *Times*, and the *East Anglian Daily Times* were, as one would expect, more restrained in tone: 'Commuter late for work halts express,' ventured the former; 'Commuters back stockbroker who flagged down a train,' offered the latter.

Neither did the ripples subside in Fleet Street. 'Irate commuter forces London express to a halt,' *South China Morning Post*. 'A wave of a brolly . . .,' The *Natal Witness*. The *Wall Street Journal* . . . well, enough is enough, and anyway by this time radio crews and television teams were beating, literally, on the doors of a house in Orvis Lane, East Bergholt. The cartoonists were enjoying a field day as well: Giles, Cookson, Mac, Maddocks — they all had a go at the Artful Dodger.

The facts of the matter, set out at the time in a written statement to the Dodger's solicitor, are as follows:

'I Francis Raymond Dodgson of Whitehayes Orvis Lane East Bergholt Suffolk Stockbroker will say as follows:—

'On Wednesday 5th March 1975 following my usual custom I arrived at Manningtree Station with a friend Mr. Robin Lingard at 07.45 with a view to catching the 07.48 train to Liverpool Street.

'The platform was crowded and at this time of day this is an indication that the earlier train which should leave Manningtree Station at 07.22 had not yet arrived. Accordingly Mr. Lingard remained in the car whilst I went to the ticket office to make enquiries. (Manningtree Station is notoriously cold and the waiting room was full.) I was told that the earlier train had broken down at Bentley thereby obstructing the 07.48, but that the earlier train would arrive in about 10 minutes (from just after 7.45) . . .

'After about a quarter of an hour a train was signalled and we got out of the car and went on the platform. It became clear that the train signalled was the Hook Continental from Parkeston Quay which normally travels non-stop to Liverpool Street. We all know this train well as it is allowed to pass through Manningtree Station before the 7.48 whenever there is a delay. It travels through the station very slowly due to the sharp bend and points before the station and a speed restriction of 10 m.p.h. There are always many empty seats on this train and it has been stopped at both Manningtree and Colchester in times of delay or emergency.

'There were no railway officials in evidence at this time so I went to the room where they normally congregate with tea and a warm fire. I found a man speaking to a railway official, presumably the official in charge. The man asked whether it was the intention to stop the Hook Continental, but the official replied that this train would not be stopped.

'This amazing show of indifference to the feelings and circumstances of the customers of British Rail appalled me, especially as some of them had been waiting for nearly an hour in the cold with as yet no correct information as to how long they might be delayed. I myself could see no prospect of getting to London at all . . .

'I left the room and by this time the train was coming round the bend to the points at the intersection before the station. The officials were either watching the train or more likely still enjoying their tea and comfort. I positioned myself in the middle of the crossing in the path of the train. This train normally accelerates from 10 m.p.h. when it is about three-quarters of the way down the platform. I had seen it come round the bend and watched it gradually approaching; when the driver reached the point where he usually accelerates he hooted. I did not know whether he had seen me or not, trains do hoot from time to time at or near the station. The light was against me so I could not see the driver through the window of his cab. I stood my ground, the driver then applied the brakes gently and the train began to stop. When it had slowed sufficiently I saw the other passengers converge on the train and open the doors. I left the crossing just before the train stopped and moved smartly on to the platform and boarded the train with the other passengers.

'At no time was there any grinding of brakes or panic, it might have been a scheduled stop at a station rather than an emergency halt. The normal main line trains frequently stop much more sharply. I have subsequently been told by a fellow passenger that he did not realise that anything untoward had happened until later.

'Whilst I stood on the crossing I remained quite motionless and at no time did I wave my arms. I was not wearing a hat and my umbrella was rolled up and packed in my brief case. I did not wave my brief case.

'After I had boarded the train there was considerable commotion with British Railways officials having at last emerged from their place of warmth and comfort. One of them recognised me and the inspector asked me to get down from the train. I did this and gave him my name and address. The driver arrived and I was verbally attacked in very strong terms personally as well for what I had done. I did not retaliate in any way. Many of the other passengers gathered round and took my part in the ensuing argument. I however took little part. I then got back on the train and the inspector told me that the police would be waiting for me at Liverpool Street.

'There was plenty of room on the train, and I was later told that it arrived only four minutes late at Liverpool Street, which is much less late than the average arrival of the 07.48.

'There were police waiting at intervals along the platform at Liverpool Street when we came in on platform 10. The impression I had was that they thought that I might make a run for it.'

Readers will observe marginal discrepancies between Mr. Dodgson's statement and certain interpretations by the media: 'A city gent,' reported the *Sun* with gusto, ' "hijacked" a boat train yesterday . . . by jumping in front of it and waving his brolly.' 'He jumped off the platform into the path of the train and waved a tightly-rolled umbrella at the driver,' commented the *Mirror*. 'City gent goes loco with the Harwich boat train . . . by flagging it down with his brief case,' reported *The Scotsman;* while *The Guardian* pointed out, with expected erudition: 'Bullfighting aficionados might, with profit, study the work of Mr. Francis Dodgson . . .'

Francis Dodgson is unlikely to do it again because, apart from all the fuss, it turned out to be an expensive business. On 3rd July 1975, at Chelmsford Crown Court, the case of Regina v Francis Raymond Dodgson came before Mr. Justice Talbot. Mr. John Samuels, defending, said: 'Given the cumulative effect of delays and frustrations which commuters from this station had to endure over the previous three or four months, there comes a time when the most civilized of men, the most social of men, does something which he might, in the cold light of dawn, realise only too well was wrong.'

To which his Lordship, sentencing, rejoined: 'Counsel invited me to view this matter in the light that, under all the circumstances which face you, and other passengers faced, that I should deal with it by way of discharge, absolute or conditional.' But, the learned judge continued, that would be as inappropriate as jailing the defendant. So he imposed a fine of £100, with £100 costs. The *Daily Express* estimated Francis Dodgson's own costs as £1,000.

At the height of the storm Francis and Anne Dodgson and their two children lived in a bungalow in Orvis Lane. Today the family, their labrador, Tara, and three cats, Sam, Smokey, and Simba, have moved into Orvis House, the family home where Francis was raised. His father farmed the land, taking the old way, preferring horses to tractors. Part of the house is 16th century, with rambling additions of 1910. They still have 100 acres, under a tenant farmer, the land reaching in front of the house, giving a sweeping view of the Stour with Mistley beyond. In the middle-ground of this rural idyll squats the villain of the piece, Manningtree Station.

It is very much a family setting: an upturned bike on the lawn, a child's swing, Tara barking, garden tools by a pond they are cleaning, a glass jug of Pimm's on a trestle table. Francis has just returned from the City, apologising for being late, 'The train, I'm afraid . . . a delay at Witham.' Anne has cooked supper; pork chops, spinach, potatoes and salad, which we eat in the garden on this early summer evening. The stillness is broken by the cry of a cock pheasant; it is broken again by a passing train.

At his trial much emphasis was given to establishing Francis Dodgson's impeccable character. The senior partner of his firm: 'reliable, resourceful and very likeable personality . . . well mannered, well educated . . . can be trusted implicitly.' A solicitor and friend of 24 years' standing: '. . . generous with his spare time . . . a thorough mixer . . .' Even the judge, in His Lordship's summing up: 'You are also a man of excellent character . . . a very useful member of society.'

Francis Dodgson is also a hard-working member of society, leaving home at 7.30 each morning, returning at 7.30 in the evening. Most days he works for half an hour in the garden, of which there are three acres, before catching his train; it is not unusual for him to remain at his office until 10.30 p.m. Two or three evenings a week are devoted to East Bergholt village affairs: he is Chairman of the cricket and hockey teams, Chairman of the Constable Hall, Vice-Chairman of the village show, financial adviser to united charities . . . when, one wonders, does this paragon have time to shave, to eat, to play with his children? Could this member of the Stock Exchange, this stalwart of village cricket, East Anglian born and bred . . . dammit, an Old Lorettonian to boot — could this be the man who, with or without brolly, hijacked the Harwich through express?

'It really wasn't premeditated at all. I was simply very angry at the negative attitude of British Rail. With a lot of others, I've been commuting 11 years and suddenly I'd had enough . . . I think perhaps it jolted them, so some good may have come of it. No, I didn't enjoy being a "cult hero" — it taught me a sharp lesson in handling the press. Never be rude to them, they can distort anything to get a good story. It made me a bit cynical.

'Commuting is worth it, yes. We lived in London in a Cheyne Walk flat at first when we married in 1965, but I always wanted to come back to Suffolk. It was financially worthwhile as well in those days — our rates were low, the fares weren't bad. Today it costs me £600 a year to get to Liverpool Street . . . that's a lot of money for an imperfect service.'

Blue-suited, modest, the epitome of the city gent

dedicated to cricket, fair play and the underdog, Francis Dodgson surveys the battlefield from his eyrie overlooking Manningtree Station. 'On balance it was probably worth it -- but I wouldn't do it again,' he says, forking up a mouthful of muscle-building spinach.

This valley of the Stour, so close to Flatford beloved of Constable and by latterday charabancs of tourists, breeds defiance. There is revolution in the slumberous Suffolk air. Randolph Churchill lived and died here . . . now there was a radical if ever there was one. Paul Jennings, living just down the way, has said his say about the countryside of his adoption:

'Why, thinks the Settler with a wild surmise,
Do natives stare at him with glassy eyes
When he, with argument and marshalled fact
Rallies them to talk no more, but act?
Perish the thought that their support is dim —
Because the charge he fights began with HIM;
Still unravished Suffolk is his hope
And he her liege, more Catholic than the Pope.'

Paul Jennings, with his hatred of land speculators and developers: 'Shoot at the tyres of their Jaguars,' once he urged.

Yes, rebellion is in the blood of these parts. Francis, with a judicial rap over the knuckles and £100 fine, copped it a bit. Consolation is that it could have been worse: section 35 of the 1861 Malicious Damage Act, under which he was charged, provides for life imprisonment.

The Blacksmith: Jim Todd

A PROUD NAME, Smith; and proud is the trade associated with such a name. Look it up in Ewan's *History of Surnames of the British Isles,* and this is what you find: 'Smith is unquestionably the greatest surname, numerically, in England and Scotland as Jones is in Wales — Murphy holding pride of place in Ireland.' It has been estimated that every 36th person in England is a Smith.

But what of the ancient craft bearing the same name; where have these Smiths gone? James Welham, the horseman, has told us that there is no longer a single horse in his village; and we shall see that Butley, which once had three blacksmiths, today has none. You can blame the motor car and the tractor, joint culprits which turned the smithy into the garage. The hiss of red-hot iron plunged into water, the ring of hammer upon anvil, the pungent smell of shoeing — these rituals have been replaced by electronic Crypton tuning, by spot welding, by 5,000 mile services. A sound horse would work for a decade at least, yet a fussy driver turns his car in after a couple of years. It is an odd kind of progress.

The blacksmith's trade may have contracted, but it is far from extinct: 'So long as there are horses, there'll be shoeing... you can do most things mechanically, but try shoeing a horse by machinery,' says Jim Todd, farrier and general smith of Great Warley, Essex. That is what is written on the sign outside the forge: 'James Todd — Farrier and General Smith.' 'Mind you,' he continues, 'there's a lot of bad shoeing done. Oh, you can tell all right — by the way a horse walks and stands. If a horse stands unlevel he'll put undue strain on tendons and ligaments. Result — lame horse. They get away with it by price-cutting and speed. Listen, it takes 40 minutes to make a pair of shoes and another 50 to shoe the horse — I get £7.50 including VAT for that, and you know nothing about the raw materials... special nails have to be imported, so we pay £6 for 5lbs., and each horse needs 28 nails. A good day is five to six horses, no more. You've never heard of a rich farrier — he earns as much as he produces.'

The forge is 130 years old, constructed of mellow brick, with a corrugated asbestos roof partly supported by a massive oak branch still with the bark on it. There are iron barred windows and great leather bellows, still used when power-cuts put the blast-blower out of action. On the coke furnace is a plaque: 'Stedall & Son. London.' There are cobwebs and grime, sparks jumping and dancing off the anvil, iron cartwheel tyres, plough-shares, horse shoes, hammers, farm implements; and, beyond the backyard, misty fields. Rain drums on the leaky roof. Terry Wogan is on Radio Two.

'Mind you,' the blacksmith says, 'I can get up to £20 a shoeing if I have to travel... more if I know they're rich.' He puts on a sly look, to let you know he is kidding. Broad-shouldered, muscular, he lifts the off-foreleg of the tethered Hackney pony, tucking it between his leather-aproned legs. 'Steady, boy,' he breathes. Long, narrow shoe nails go through the horn hoof to the outside and turn over in a clench. Jim straightens them, draws them out: off comes the shoe. He brings out a knife, paring the bottom of the hoof. He goes to the forge, picking out a white-hot shoe and cools it in the water tank. That acrid smell again and clouds of smoke as the shoe is fitted. The shoe is whipped back to the fire, reheated, clapped on the anvil, hammered into shape; finally it is cooled and nailed on. A couple of pairs of new shoes, bespoke, made-to-measure; with normal use they will last five weeks or so.

Behind a glass case are certificates and ribbons: 'This is to certify that D.A. Todd has passed a practical test in oxy-acetylene welding in accordance with the syllabus of the Rural Industries Bureau — 1st September 1948.' Next to it is a replica certificate made out in the name of J. Todd, dated 10th February 1965. There is a certificate of merit from the London Harness Horse Parade Society, presented by *Horse & Hound* to James Todd for 'Efficient Shoeing'. Ribbons — from fourth to Champion — awarded by the Essex County Show, the Colchester Horse Society.

'I was born at Danbury in 1945,' Jim says. 'We moved to Tyler's Hall Farm at Great Warley, my father was cowman there... but grandpa was a farrier in the 1914

War. It was Uncle David who took over the forge, and I always used to go and watch him, every day on my way to the village school... I'd always wanted to work with animals, it was being brought up on a farm. I wanted to go to him as an apprentice, but the apprenticing body wouldn't accept me for three years — too many applicants. But eventually I served my four years with Uncle David as my master... but I passed my Registered Shoeing Smith exam after one year, so I hadn't been wasting time.

'I stayed with my uncle 13 years, until he retired five years ago, then I took over, renting the forge from him. I've got two apprentices of my own now, and an assistant, Paul Atkins. About nine lads apply each year to me — well, the nearest forge is at Basildon. Not many in Norfolk and Suffolk... there's a good few hunts here, let's see... the Essex Union, Essex Farmers, the Essex, East Essex — a mass of pony clubs too.' (James Wentworth Day, a veteran horseman who once made a record ride of 1,340 miles on a horse through East Anglia, estimated in 1974 that there were about 400,000 horses in Britain, numbers increasing yearly. 'About 1,200 shoeing smiths look after them,' he wrote. 'We need at least 1,500.')

Jim Todd is powerfully built. He says that his job is not a question of muscle — but it obviously helps. He is good-looking in the way of the male model you see on the hoardings, sweaty-browed after felling a couple of hundred trees, slaking his thirst on Harp Lager. His sideburns are long, bushy, his jaw slightly prognathous. One suspects that he is no prolific reader of Stendhal, but that he does not have trouble in attracting women. He bends over the anvil with concentration, unflinching as the sparks fly. Probably he is physically fearless, determined, usually getting his own way. He seems more determined than sensitive; there can be few grey areas in his life.

'Muscle? That's a myth. It's patience you need when you're working with animals — and a good eye to see that a horse stands level. The priority is shoeing, that's my favourite job, what I like doing. It's the contact — there's something between you and a horse, a sense, a horse can tell if you know what you're doing. What other job's like that? A horse can tell if a farrier's using too heavy a hammer... I've shod horses that are reputedly unshoeable, ones other farriers won't touch. There was this coloured mare that five farriers refused to shoe, no one could do a thing with her. She came in here and I put a twitch on her...well, she reared and her eyes came out on organ stops. I talked to her, talked to her all the time, comforting her until she went out like a puppy. Some farriers can't talk to horses. I sometimes wonder why they do it at all... it's like a racing driver not knowing what's under the bonnet.

'But these days I've had to learn to deal, be tougher... I'm tougher than my competitors, so I'm more successful. Put it this way: five years ago I had nothing — now I'm buying a house, I own the forge. You know my ambition?' He hangs on to it a moment, creating an effect of drama. 'I'd like to own all the property along this road... well, it's what it's all about, isn't it? I'll get there too — I'm on my way.

'We're doing a lot of agricultural repair work as well. Farmer Jones' hay-cutting machine breaks down... well, you make hay while the sun shines, the weather won't wait. It's got to be fixed at once, not next week. Like with a milking-parlour if the equipment breaks down — you can't leave cattle unmilked. Harvest... combines go wrong, straw-baling machines... all got to be working again in no time at all. Parts wear and fracture with machinery, you'd be surprised. With shoeing now, Christmas is our busy time. There's the Christmas Eve meet, Boxing Day, the children's holidays at Pony Club. I'm working five and a half days a week from 7.30 a.m. until 10.15 p.m.

'No, I'm not married. I'm courting pretty heavily... mother lives with me since we lost father last year. She cooks and makes my bed, that's all — I'm never there. I've no luxuries, I skip all that and I don't care much. I'd like to have more time to ride, but it's my own fault if I press too hard — I can see myself pressing all my life. I've got to... I see myself as about the same standard as a vet, but I don't make what a vet makes.'

Colonel L— calls in at the forge at that moment, handing Jim a buff envelope. They talk for a few minutes, Jim addressing his visitor as 'Colonel'. 'Every year at this time he comes in with two tickets to the Royal International Horse Show at Wembley. I remember shoeing a mare called Ditchling for him once... he had this ambition to hunt on his 70th birthday. But when the day came there was no hunting around. Didn't put him off, he hacked miles and miles to an adjoining hunt to get his day out.'

Jim Todd is not modest by nature, but neither is he immodest. He is his own man and he did not attend charm school to learn to be himself. Take me or leave me, that is his attitude; he has no special airs for special customers. But what he doesn't tell you is that he really does have to be a bit of a vet. He must know the seven bones of a horse's leg below the knee — cannon or short bone, long and short pastern, coffin bone, navicular and two sessamoids. He understands their functions and how to deal with them. Equally he knows the effects of foot diseases: ring-bone, side-bone, spavins, capped elbows, curbs, navicular disease. They demand refined shoeing, including surgical shoes of odd shapes to offset the damage done by disease. He has mentioned none of this.

Another ambition is that he would like to breed horses; and you can see that he means this more than his intention of becoming a man of property. Talking about horses, he becomes alive; discussing his proposed 'property deals' he begins to sound like an advertisement in one of the Sunday supplements.

'Are women like horses? That's a naughty question — that's naughty. The girl I'm courting now . . . I don't know what I look for. I'd never go for a show animal, they're useless outside the ring. Take a pretty one and you learn the truth later — but if there's no flash, there's no personality.

'I got saddled up with a fiery little mare a while back, but that didn't last . . .'

The Publican: Vera Sybil Noble

BUTLEY is a plain Jane village. An unchivalrous thing to say, but it is so. There is something of the spinster in her demeanour. Once perhaps, she was frivolous, a flirt; once, perhaps, she had a love, lost to a shallow grave in Flanders mud. Maybe his name was Ashkettle, Hazelwood, Mann, Pettitt, or Smith — all inscribed on the Great War Roll of Honour in the Church of St. John the Baptist. On the other hand, perhaps it was the 20's and 30's, the depressed years, which gave her this calloused look.

To the stranger, Butley remains inaccessible, manacled to a past which saw more poverty than gaiety. To this day, smiles are rare in Butley. It is a village, says the rector, David Wall, that visitors drive through on the way to somewhere else. There is, the rector continues, a move to revive the community; but the energy comes from newcomers rather than those born and bred here. Newcomers such as Richard Newnham who runs the youth club, and Vic Harrap who has started a fund to restore the village hut. There are a few renovated cottages, the 'second homes' of city week-enders; but their owners are mostly quiet, not given to making a fuss. Butley is no place for stockbrokers fertilizing their friendships in jolly Sunday morning martini rites.

The land is light, so that high winds claw at it, dragging it across the road into rippling dunes. Hedges are cut low, so that you can see across fields into the forests of Tunstall and Rendlesham: dark as sin those forests are, and full of fearsome tales. Up Short Walk are the council houses, sulphurous yellow in aspect; and tucked away at the back, so that cabbage patch meets asphalt playground, is Butley C of E Middle School constructed, so it seems, of glass and wood and a prayer that it will all hold together. Children in green jerseys play there; children from Campsey Ash, Iken, Bawdsey and Orford — yet few from Butley.

It was not always so. Six Pettitts went to the Kaiser's

War, three Manns, five Hazelwoods, and enough Smiths to make sure the Hun kept his head down. There were eight Hazelwood children, five boys and three girls. Wesley Hazelwood, now 82, lives with his sister Isabel in the Post Office and General Stores... only you cannot buy a postal order or a packet of Daz today; they were closed up back in 1974. Wesley juts his jaw out when he speaks: he fought through the Somme, Vimy Ridge, Ypres, and was wounded three times before he caught his Blighty one — enough of a thump that was to send him back to work the land that reared him.

Isabel has photographs of them all at school. Demure children, they look, in their Sunday best, squatting at teacher's feet; and not a smile between them, even then. She has a post-card of the village street, taken at the turn of the century when the old Queen wasn't much longer for this world. 'We all kept a pig in the backyard,' she recalls. 'We killed two a week to sell in the shop. There were three blacksmiths in the village, and a shoemaker. There's not a single shop today — they deliver twice a week by van... and there's two buses a day to Woodbridge.' More photographs, one of a blacksmith posing sheepishly by a horse he is shoeing. A bright fire burns in the grate; and Wesley's long johns are steaming from a clothes' horse. There is a colour television in the corner which they eye from time to time, as if expecting an important personal communication.

'You get all the news soon as it happens,' explains Wesley. 'We didn't know the Great War was over... we heard them singing up at the Oyster, so we went to see for ourselves. They were singing because the Germans had surrendered.'

Next door to the Hazelwoods, at number 9, The Street, lives Butley's senior citizen, Mr. Large, a widower of 97 years, spry and bright as a jackdaw. He is famous, naturally, since the *East Anglian Daily Times* came along to take his picture. 'They wanted me in the paper, asked a lot of questions — it's all here, you see. I suppose it's because there's not many of us left — they've all gone, the old ones, all dead. Place is full of strangers these days — and those aeroplanes buzzing around. I go to bed early, but they wake me up...buzz, buzz, buzz. 'Course I remember the old Queen, Queen Victoria. I wasn't well at the time and when the doctor came to see me he said: "Well, the Queen's dead — things'll change from now on." He was right, eh? Oh, I enjoy myself. I'll make it to a hundred. Got to — this Queen will write me a letter. Or I might go to where she lives: Crystal Palace ... no, no, *Buckingham* Palace. She might give me a medal.'

Just up the road is the Oyster, where everyone sang the evening peace returned to Butley in 1918. It sells Adnams beer, packets of crisps, Polo peppermints and chocolate bars. None of your shepherd's pie or ploughman's lunch. The ploughman, Jimmy Clark, brings his own lunch: sandwiches and a jammy wedge of Lyons Swiss Roll which he eats by a slow-drawing fire over a pint of mild. He has worked on the same farm for 47 years. 'Why's it called the Oyster? Don't rightly know, but I've been turning over oyster shells for years. Turning 'em over and ploughing 'em back in. They're all over the fields. Reckon they came from the oyster beds in the river.' He says it is not especially good land, light and sandy as it is. Mostly the crops are carrots, corn, sugar beet, with some beans towards the water. Apart from the Adnams carrier, he is the only noon-time customer.

Vera Sybil Noble is the tenant. Her father was before her, and his father before that. Sixty glorious years between them. She makes a living because: 'I do it all myself. I don't pay anyone, that's where the profit goes. It used to be called The Green Shutters years ago, but then they started to do oyster suppers ... I think that's what it was.' She is part of this place, three generations part of it; almost as much part, you could say, as the great beams holding it together. Yet she talks in a way which makes one feel she is a stranger herself, passing through.

The Butley Oyster is set at a fork in the road, pink-washed and squat. There is nothing glamorous about it. You would not expect to find model girls in sheer hose, drinking Babycham with lean men in blazers. There are rough wooden tables and chairs, three or four sepia-tinted photos of the steel quoits team and the football team. The walls and ceiling are sepia-tinted too, with years of tobacco smoke ingrained into the fabric. There are no horse brasses and hunting horns, no fairy lights, no photographs of mine host clasped in Bruce Forsyth's sincere embrace. There is precious little bad language either; or smutty stories. Vera

Noble (how impossible it is to guess her age) looks as if she would stand no nonsense.

There is, however, a notice in her bar: *'Nowadays one lives in terror of fine country pubs being "tarted up", but the Oyster has not had a penny misspent on it either by the brewer or the landlady. The company to be found in it are foresters and farm-workers and there you will hear the purest coastal Suffolk, the sweetest English you will hear in any town. If the seeker wishes to find the heart of East Anglia he must know the East Anglian countryman. On a fine summer evening you may be lucky at Butley to see the old game of quoits. The quoit is of steel, and heavy, flung at a long distance into a pad of clay. "Freehand written by Bob Hart, aged 79."'*

Bob Hart was a regular. Vera keeps a sketch of him propped up against some empty crates behind the counter. Someone has drawn him, in heavy pencil or charcoal, together with his mates — Percy Webb, Dick and Ernie Birch, and Cecil Ellis. 'Dead,' says Vera, 'all of them dead. I told you it was a dying village. You won't see many children about today. There's some young people come on Sunday from miles away, all over. That's our busy evening, Sunday, we're always packed because of the folk music in the parlour. I didn't used to like it, being on a Sunday, but beggars can't be choosers.

'Bob Hart and Percy Webb, they'd sing *The Gypsy's Warning, Seventeen Come Sunday, John Barleycorn.* There might be a fiddle or a squeeze box, a guitar ... always someone doing something. No, never any trouble — never in my lifetime, even in the War.

'Yes, the brewery was good to us in the War. We got our quota; some spirits too. We'd open from midday to 1 pm and then from eight to 10 pm, and there'd always be a queue ... our own soldiers, the Irish, Americans. Four bombs dropped on us one night, in 1941 it was, all in that field there. Mrs. Caley was bathing her baby and a bit of shrapnel came and smashed her window — that shook her. But the war was the good times here ... apart from people getting killed.

'It was a peaceful place them days. Did I tell you Margaret Catchpole and the smugglers came here? Changed now, those American planes making all that noise; and the bombs, we see bombs big as this, on trailers going by at night. I'd like to see them all pack up and go. It makes us a target if it starts again. And they don't come to the Oyster — they slip up to London in them big cars, very likely.'

It is a confusing time for the remaining souls in the parish of Butley. They belong to the past, not the future; and this bewilders them. Three smithies have closed because there are no horses to shoe; the post office has gone, so too the grocer and the shoemaker. Progress has besieged Butley. So the villagers turn inwards upon themselves, suspecting that the world is going mad and that they have been abandoned. Supersonic fighters scream overhead, grey bats out of hell; and bombs are ferried along the street at night. This peace seems more dangerous than their war.

The Nun: Sister Judith Mary Cuff

SISTER JUDITH is headmistress of a small independent grammar school for girls between the ages of five and 16. Although the school is in Ipswich, Sister Judith lives in a community, the Sisters of Jesus and Mary, in a terraced house behind the Regal Cinema in Stowmarket. She was herself educated at the same school where she now teaches, the sisters having a significant influence upon her decision to join the Order herself.

The headmistress's study at the school is functional: an uncluttered desk, three or four chairs, a safe, bookcase, crucifix. It is ordered, calm: *There all things are waxen neat, And set in decorous lines* ... She sits upright, smoothing her habit unselfconsciously. She looks younger than her 42 years and this youthfulness has nothing to do with Elizabeth Arden beauty products.

She smiles and laughs gently at each question. She uses expressions like 'blowing my top' and 'hang ups' quite often. She says 'one' frequently: 'One applies to the bursar for shopping money.' Around her neck hangs a crucifix and, because she is married to Christ, there is a gold band on the third finger of her left hand. In her study seems less bigotry, less intransigence than in *Coronation Street*. Standing up, walking across a courtyard, she becomes uncertain, almost gauche. Perhaps it is because of her height: she is almost six feet tall. There is a stillness and a certainty which nothing on this earth, death least of all, could violate.

'One never knows how it all started. At school here I was aware that the sisters had access to a scale of values which were different to those of post-war Britain. I was attracted to it although I couldn't have put this attraction into words. Then came a basic decision — my vocation or marriage to someone I'd been going out with a long time.

'My religious vocation is simply to search for the ultimate meaning, truth and beauty, and try to keep an ultimate purpose always to the front of my life. In practical terms it's spelt out in the amount of time we give to prayer and the structure of our lives which is summed up in those vows of poverty, chastity, and obedience. My work in running the school is on the grounds of complete parity between academic and spiritual training.'

Of East Anglia's religious persuasion: 'There's always been a nonconformist tradition because East Anglia has tended to be on the margin of the established church. It's always been idiosyncratic... one is always aware of the forces operating in the nonconformist traditions; and how easily it merges into something that's akin to folklore and superstition — the dividing lines aren't too clearly drawn. On Sunday the chapels are fuller; the Anglican churches vary, but I imagine statistically would be emptier than churches in much of Britain. The Catholic church — again, emptier. The idiosyncratic factions, as I've called them, might have come about because isolated communities had such remote contact with the established church through history — but that's my own reading into it. A bit like Laurie Lee... incest flourishing where communications were bad!

'I chose a teaching order because, as someone born and bred in Ipswich, I was aware that there was something wider than Ipswich... and I wanted to share this breadth of vision with others.'

Sister Judith is conscious of the differences between children of indigenous Suffolk families and children of town families; the gap widening in cases where family commitments are totally to the city: 'Thinking of one child I teach... she comes from a well established farming background, her references are to the soil of Suffolk and her reactions are slower. No, I wouldn't use the word "retarded", I'd simply say *slower* because I suspect quicksilver thinking — there's so much in our culture which is encouraging people to think too quickly, and they have pre-packaged sets of words which they use to a prescribed formula. One suspects the amount of thought which presents the package. So I have more faith in the slower Suffolk reponse, because it's been thought out and is more profound. The city child tends to respond more quickly but, it seems to me, superficially and artificially — and you can predict what they're going to do or say.

'One wouldn't want to make a blanket statement, but

the country children — well, many of them — are up very early, exercising their ponies, mucking out their rabbits and guinea pigs. They're in touch with nature, other values, for perhaps an hour morning and evening — and they're in bed earlier, while the town child is watching television . . . which becomes her frame of reference. The country child, through involvement with nature and farm life, is often more able to shoulder responsibility — I think I'd put it in those terms rather than the old concept of the family sitting around the hearth enjoying musical evenings or Monopoly.

'We suffer in the school from the child who becomes immersed in what the town provides for adolescents — it's damaging, if not positively destructive. I'm thinking of one or two 14 and 15 year olds who have become so infected by the people they've come into contact with that their only object in life is to make a name for themselves in some form of canned entertainment of the most trivial variety. It's sad, particularly when it happens to an intelligent girl who has been blinded by this set of values. The youth culture is so developed that many town parents opt out of providing an enriching background for the children . . . so the temptation for the child is to accept what is offered.'

A child's sense of perspective is a delicate mechanism, readily blurred by the antics of its parents. Bidden to do so, a circus bear will roll over on his back, legs ludicrously in the air; some human adults perform in the same manner if social pressures so dictate.

'There are some parents who are totally town orientated, but live in splendidly renovated cottages, bringing themselves to Ipswich in one of the family cars; but their relationship with the countryside is negligible. The point being, I suppose, that it's chic, is it, to have a country address? So there are people with a Suffolk address because it means something in a certain environment; but I wouldn't imagine they have any deeper contact with the soil than driving past the beauty of the countryside.'

Thus far Sister Judith offers little comfort; her attitudes suggest that she is fighting a losing battle: 'To try to give you a real answer, I think we're on a watershed now. There are still at the top of the school the end of the generation who have inherited the culture of the sixties, believing that the world owes them a living and that they have a right to whatever they want. They are anti-authoritarian, exceedingly materialistic . . . whereas you've got another set, and obviously there's no strict dividing line, influenced by current society — aware that they are unlikely to get jobs, aware that graduate qualifications are a ticket to nothing at all. They are influenced by a different form of religious practice — we can at least interest them today when it would have provoked hysterical laughter a few years ago. I'm happier to see children with a more realistic approach to life, less affected by adolescent cultures. But youth as a whole is much as it always has been. The basic material doesn't change — the pressures and criteria of society do.'

The future . . . 10 years' time? 'I wish I knew. Underlying all this is the political question — will a school like this be given the opportunity to survive and will the economic climate allow parents to support such schools? Given these things, then my guess, my hunch, is that the formal and spiritual sides of education will come very close together indeed. Again, I feel that the comprehensive school will go from strength to strength, therefore the values that we offer here will have to be found within the family and the parish. My personal view is that we shall ultimately have a partial dismantling of the present system, with due importance being given to the other agencies which incarnate — in that sort of language — values which larger comprehensives cannot offer — whereas smaller communities may find themselves better equipped for inculcating human values . . . and your wheel comes full circle then with people back in their churches because they're nice, cosy communities!'

Despite chic addresses and the Jaguar syndrome, the townsman's 'status' does not, in Sister Judith's view, seem to impress the countryman unduly: 'The countryman is proud and happy to be of the country. Very much so, even in my own family my sister is always commenting adversely on my parents' determination to live in the town. So far as the children are concerned it's the other way round: the town girl pities the country girl, looks down on her slightly if we're using this kind of terminology, because they haven't got the same opportunities to enjoy the more fun aspects of Ipswich —

those aspects which I've said can be corrupting.

'One of our precise problems is that so many of the children have got all the material possessions they want. What else *can* they want? Well, when they realise that they don't want anything else, but that they need *something*... in theory that's where we step in, but that's a very adult reaction and only the more sensitive reach that stage here. We've reached the point where we've become satiated with possessions — and being satiated implies the closeness of an emetic... or a Reformation. I would say that the majority of our more intelligent girls, middle and older girls, have a huge question mark over the future, but it's nothing they can be articulate about. Yes, it concerns them; and it even frightens some of them because they can see a possibility of, say, the Third World rising up and depriving them of some of the possessions they have come to depend on. They fear that life might become uncomfortable and nasty; a few even fear for their safety.'

(This indictment of something very close to amorality is a pessimistic statement — and one which I personally do not accept as being typical, or consistent with Sister Judith's general view of society. A few months before this particular conversation, Sister Judith and I were talking of other matters; inevitably, we got around to the 'state of the world'. Her comments are before me as I write: 'I do not believe,' she told me, 'that our society is more acquisitive, cruel, greedy than in the past. The documentation happens to be different. In the mid-19th century we relied on Dickens to tell us what was going on. Now it's opinion polls. What I regret most is the effect the mass media has in forming attitudes.

'I'm optimistic enough to believe that there will be a levelling out of standards of living across the world, and that for us living in the developed areas will mean a levelling down, an awareness that the acquisition of goods in material terms is no longer the goal.')

These almost diametrically opposed opinions, only go to illustrate Sister Judith's suspicion of words: 'I have a profound distrust of words. What you use in their place I don't know. Words, with teaching children, are supposed to be base tools — and they're showing themselves to be inefficient. I don't know the answer. We must grope.

'I believe there is too much talk in the world — we've

been over-exposed to chatter and have thus lost the meaning of words for genuine communication. The value of silence is that it brings one back to oneself because everything else in our culture tends to encourage us to turn outwards — whereas silence brings you back to yourself. By silence I mean interior silence, a sort of silence which is attempting to reach a state of total silence in every part of our being. Silence is a strength which most of us are too weak to have.'

The Sportsman: James Wentworth Day

HE WILL NOT love me for saying so, but my old friend James Wentworth Day is running behind a little these days. Hardly surprising, if he will get up to pranks that would daunt a man a quarter his age. Take this latest escapade. Down at the Ingatestone pub, not far from his Victorian 'Early Gas Age' house. They were discussing strength in the bar parlour that evening; strength and the weight a man can lift. James said he could easily lift the heaviest man in the room — a 16 stoner — and being the sportsman he is, laid a wager on it.

He lifted the man all right; then, to prove his point, he made to walk a few steps. It was his undoing. He tripped and fell, 16 stone of human dumb-bell on top of him. The impact burst his bladder. A doctor gave him three months to live but James, considering that there was still a drop or two of drinkable claret left in the world, that East Anglian sunsets were getting no less majestic, that there were still a few game birds to shoot.... well, all these things considering, and a few more besides, he decided he might as well live. Which is precisely what he did.

Unquenchably, there is the spirit of the 'Fen-Tiger' in him; their blood is in his veins for in 1899 he was born at the Marsh House at Exning, Newmarket, where he was Lord of the Manors of Exning Hall and Landwade Hall. He is proud that he has kept one foot in a marsh and the other in a duck-punt since his earliest days. He is proud too of the pugilistic quality of the pre-1914 Fenman: 'Your true Fenman loves a scrap. If he can bust up his neighbours' village feast at the peak of its gaiety, he is delighted. They fought with fists, sticks, hobnailed boots. Why, the villages of Wicken and Soham were practically in a state of war. Law? Fen Tigers made their own laws ... they killed the first village policeman. Hit him over the head and stuck his body in a lime kiln. Never did catch the culprits. At Wicken, where I lived with my mother, she was the village

Florence Nightingale — all the boys touched their caps to her, as I was taught to touch mine to the humblest village woman. We had candlelight and oil, no telephone, no doctor — he'd arrive by gig if he was needed. We had spring water; the best I've drunk in my life. Yes, there was inbreeding, but not much dottiness.

'Lots of suspicion though — suspicious of strangers the Fenman is, but absolutely trustworthy to his own sort. We were Tory and High Church . . . we inherited that from the Puritans. There were five Cromwells buried in the churchyard.'

He recalls a Fenman of his youth. Uriah Marshall was his name: 'He was short, swarthy and thickset, with bright gipsy eyes and a soul packed with guile. He wore gold ear-rings, a peaked cap, a seaman's pea jacket, moleskin waist-coat and trousers of some strange old fustian material. He was the Lothario of the village belles, a great fighter when the beer was in him, an invincible snapper up of hares and rabbits and the nimblest bird catcher for miles around. I adored him. He was my boyhood hero.

'Ury slept, ate, cooked and seldom washed in one big room. His bed hid behind a filthy curtain. A stuffed cormorant, a barn owl, a case of wooden-looking French partridges, and a stuffed hawk or two lulled his slumbers. You could cut the smell with a knife. His only weapon was a walking stick. He never used a 12 bore. "Guns is fer gennelmen and fules," he impressed on me. "I gits me buds quick and nat'ral. Why, bless yer, young Master Wentworth, the little old bewties don't know I've ketched 'em till they're in me nets." Ury was the greatest poacher for miles around.'

In the words of H.T. Massingham, James Wentworth Day was 'born and bred in the true tradition of the 18th century sportsmen-naturalists'. But with no private fortune JWD had to choose a career: he chose journalism. He spent early formative years as a right-hand man to the late Lord Beaverbrook, and later helped to edit *Country Life:* 'I missed the editorship because I told the then editor that he used his title as a way of getting into stately homes that wouldn't allow him through the door any other way.' Since then he has edited *The Field, The Illustrated Sporting and Dramatic News, The Saturday Review* and *English Life.*

He has fought two parliamentary elections as a High

Tory. He won a political libel action in the High Courts which made legal history. He has helped to organise an Everest expedition, completed a 7,000 mile survey of Newfoundland and untrodden Labrador, has written 'intimate' biographies of King George V, the Queen Mother, Princess Marina, Duchess of Kent. In all he has published 'between 47 and 50 books' — he has not kept totally accurate records. His mental inventory of personal effects is more reliable: '400 stuffed birds and animals, 53 guns, 110 antique chairs, several stags' heads, a portrait of my ancestor Thomas Wentworth, 1st Earl of Strafford — so real that when I've drunk enough port I talk to it — a valuable collection of pewter, a hell of a lot of books, one wife. I picked her up at a bus stop in Piccadilly, made her share my taxi and hijacked her to The Savoy for lunch. She told me she worked in a store and I said it must be Fortnum and Mason because it was the only shop in London to employ ladies. I was right.'

One wonders if he used similar piratical methods in ensnaring others of his many friends. People like the late Lady Houston, reputedly the richest person in England at a time when she made JWD her personal representative. Or Alexander George Francis Drogo Montagu, 10th Duke of Manchester, who died in November 1977, thus ending a 50 years friendship with James. Then came his Essex friends, from Mersea, Brittlesea, from the Crouch and the Roach, from Tollesbury and Maldon, bearing names less ducal and quicker to the point. Such as Art Bugg, 'Councillor', of whom Mrs. Bungo Blow, wife of the landlord of the *Nelson's Eye* remarked: 'Sich language I never did hear. Comin' from a man on the Council too.'

James remembers his companions of long ago: there was Bob Simpkin, known as Bob Fal-Lal since he declared that he was 'no townboy but a pore simple owd Fen-Tiger, with no fal-lals about me.' Clearly, JWD recalls, he was 'one of the Saxon "Kin of Sim"; and Sim like enough came up our East Anglian rivers with beak-prowed longship, banked oars thrashing, the deep sides of the well of the ship glittering with shields, the Raven of Odin at the mast-head and the wild, wild war cry of "Yuch! Hey! Saa-Saa" going before them on the wind — the blood-curdling cry of the Viking invaders.'

There was Joe Phypers, 'small, wizened, brown as a

berry, quick as a weasel who rubbed goose grease into his skin to keep fen mists and ague at bay.' Bob King was a man of 'simple philosophy, with a great faith in God'. When they had Bandy Matches (an ancient form of ice hockey) on Spinney Fen, Bob would recount how 'harf a score o' min lam each other on the shins with their sticks, and kick each other till they fell down and had to be tuk home on turf barrows'.

The amazing Dr. John Henry Salter from the Essex village of Tolleshunt D'Arcy, was another friend. Born in 1841, he died at 90 in 1932, and during his life-time owned 2,696 dogs of which he bred 2,123 himself. Between 1865 and 1925 he shot 62,504 head of game and wildfowl — 11 wolves, shot in Russia, were part of his bag. He won 1,400 prizes for fruit, flowers and vegetables. He brought more than 10,000 Essex babies into the world.

Dr. Salter's diary relates that on Christmas Eve 1920 he was up at 4 am, down on the flooded marsh, up to his knees in water 'with an east wind blowing strong and rain in torrents' and records that he fell into deep mud and water 'shooting under the worst circumstances of weather from 5 to 10 am, a walk of the beastliest description for 8 miles and then 50 miles patient-seeing afterwards... a good wholesome day for a young man of 80'. There are no references in the youthful doctor's diary to weight-lifting contests in public houses.

And what about 'Admiral' Bill Wyatt 'that artist among shipwrights who, when 80, would tell you that he could ride a bicycle to London, walk 10 miles, drink a gallon of ale, ride a donkey, build a boat, shoot a duck — and sail and win a race in his 50 year old smack *Unity*. A man indeed!'

It seems a fierce, competitive business, being a companion of James Wentworth Day's. And yet: 'Go to the Norfolk Broads in spring when the brown winter reeds turn to tender green and cattle marshes are lit by the brassy glint of marsh marigolds and gentle cuckoo flowers. Then redshanks ring their carillon of ariel bells and courting snipe plunge earthwards... bitterns boom on indigo nights under the stars. They, like the Great Bustard, were extinct when many of us were boys... and the weeping, wailing plover, the clanking, mad-headed coots, comfortable mallards and jewelled teal, with a host of other wildfowl, make the music and the magic of Broadland in spring, autumn and winter when trippers have folded their tents and stowed away their fancy hats and gone home to the cinema and the telly.' How he hates trippers, 'long haired louts', and town hall bureaucrats. To say nothing of weekend shooters from London — 'marsh cowboys'. He positively bristles with malevolence; the Fen-Tiger sharpening his claws.

No, he is not a modern man. Times have changed and he is not entirely in sympathy with the process: 'I regret the break up of the estates, the days of feudalism which also contained a high sense of duty, and the passing of the small village manor whose squire worked his own acres — they used to say that the master's foot was the best dung on the land. I suppose there are blessings . . . higher wages, social security which has wiped out the acute fear of the workhouse. The motor car helps get produce to market quickly and the telephone is a blessed instrument. Can't stand pop festivals, cheapjack clothing and American gadgets. Abroad? Abroad is bloody.'

His idols are not today's idols, whom he considers tarnished and rather vulgar. His heroes are men of the land, sportsmen like himself, men who would take up arms for a cause and, as in the case of his own ancestor Thomas Wentworth, put his head on the block for a loyalty. Men like Tom de Grey, 5th Lord Walsingham, who 'in the days when big bags were in fashion, broke the world's record by killing 1,070 grouse in a day, using 1,510 cartridges.' Men like Coke of Norfolk, 'Turnip' Townshend, men he has shot with, fished with, fought with, by whose sides he has ridden.

He admires buildings such as Raynham, which 'centres round a singularly beautiful house of Jacobean gaiety and classic purity, an example of Inigo Jones at his pioneering best'. He is in reverence of the Priory of St. Osyth, 'perhaps the finest monastic building in East Anglia'. He is less ecstatic about Norwich City Hall, 'which has the proportions of a brick and the complexion of Brown Windsor soup'.

His outspokenness has made him a controversial figure, has earned him enemies. He seems indifferent to this, his tacit statement being that a man should be faithful to his principles and that if the rest of the world doesn't like it then let the rest of the world go hang itself. His feeling for East Anglia is passionate; his feeling for London is equally passionate, siding with the Norfolker who said: 'Why goo to London, tha's a mucky owd hole.' He is still scarred by the years he spent in 'refined poverty' in London at a time when the family fortunes took a turn for the worse. It was an exile he found hard to bear.

Not long ago I asked what possessions he would like to take into the next world; two possessions I offered him, a sound and a sight. He chose Alfred Munning's autobiography, and his favourite gun, a double barrelled Purdey 20 bore, about 70 years old with Damascus barrels. His sound was the call of the curlew. His sight was 'my own Adventure Fen lying between Reach and Burwell Lodes as it was before drainage, when you could see hundreds of wildfowl in the air.'

I do not believe James Wentworth Day thinks much about death and if, in moments of port-induced reverie, he ever does he probably views it in bucolic terms... St. Peter, dressed in plus-fours and Norfolk jacket, a 12 bore under his arm, instructing angelic beaters to put up a covey of celestial grouse so that everyone can have a bit of sport.

The Nurse: Kay Pargeter

AT ADDENBROOKE'S HOSPITAL, Cambridge, there is no such thing as a new day, because the old one never ended. Where sickness and healing are concerned, day and night are indistinguishable. There is simply a moment of revitalization as night staff prepare to hand over to day staff.

During the next 24 hours many hundreds of feet will tread the Out-Patients Department carpet, ambulances will make 30 emergency calls, 96 casualties will be treated by the Accident Service. Throughout the hospital 2,287 staff will support 800 bed patients costing the National Health Service £43.77 for each patient day.

Many patients will be admitted and many, after an average stay of nine days, will be discharged; some will undergo major surgery; a few will be told that their condition is inoperable and will face the verdict with courage, fear, even disbelief. Amputees will learn to take their first steps with false limbs; previously independent spirits may sense humiliation because they can no longer control bodily functions; there will be renewed pain for some, fresh hope for others. Some patients will receive flowers and visitors; others will face the day alone. One young man will not even realise that another day has dawned, because he has not regained consciousness since he was admitted months ago. Several patients will die, some of them fighting like the devil, others slipping away with gratitude.

In Ward D.8 — General Surgery - the Staff Nurse is handing over her night duty notes to the day staff under a Sister. Breakfast is being served from trolleys to the 26 ward patients. As Staff Nurse leaves to return to her flat in the Residence, Sister gathers her day team around her for briefing. Note books are open: 'Two men coming in . . . now you know how important it is for a diabetic to look after his feet . . . she has a big lump, you can almost shake hands with it . . . she's only 25 and nervous, so she'll ask a lot of questions . . . Mr. Vickers is due for his pre-med., he'll go down to the theatre at 9.30, they're going to take a look at his abdomen ... Mrs. Kent has terrible wind, but she relieved herself ... green sputum ... quite a lot of pus, not draining properly ... she is completely incontinent ... Mrs. Jackson's still on her refusing lark, refusing all tablets ....'.

Mr. Yates is a patient in this ward. He is 70 and underwent recent surgery for carcinoma of the rectum. In three days will be the next operation, closure of a temporary colostomy, which should see him fit again: 'They're pleased with my internal plumbing. No, I don't get nervous ... look, in 1915 I had my appendix out and a bloody great scar it left. My son had his out and you can hardly see the scar. Progress! What a stinking job these young nurses have, but they're so cheerful ... make us feel loved ... I'm not contributing any more, but they don't make me feel guilty. They make me feel proud, human, not a useless old man. I saw India, China ... the army. Seen the workhouse too ... used to wash jam jars and sell them for a farthing apiece. They weren't the good old days ... these are the good days. I get a bit emotional when I talk about these nurses ... they make me feel that this is the time to be living.'

'That's really what nursing is all about,' says Sister Kay Pargeter. 'Loving and caring — common sense and kindness in a way. I'm lucky because I've never been squeamish, I've never minded clearing away other people's messes. I enjoy basic nursing — washing, cleaning, feeding, the physical contact with patients. I used to hate giving injections in case it caused pain — you wonder about that until you've had experience — but I'm never worried about the mess a human can make. They can't help it and it upsets them more than it does us. A nurse should never make a patient feel embarrassed to ask for a bedpan. Sometimes it upsets a young student nurse of 18, they get frightened — and then they learn. They blossom as they learn, it's lovely to see. Qualifications and A-levels are fine with students, but first they need loving kindness.'

Kay Pargeter is a Cambridge girl, born in the Romsey Old Town district 38 years ago. She was one of six children, daughter of a baker. With so many children her mother had little time for anything other than housekeeping. They were a tightly-knit family, self-sufficient, old fashioned and 'ordinary'. Kay uses the word 'ordinary' about herself frequently: 'I didn't dream I could be a nurse — I had no qualifications, only a secondary education. I was very ordinary.'

She cannot remember when she first wanted to nurse, but recalls admiring the neighbouring women in their street; women with precious little instruction, yet who always knew how to deliver a baby, how to lay out the dead. At 10 she joined the Red Cross to learn rudimentary first-aid, graduating eventually to Senior Red Cross. She had a bad stutter and children gave her a hard time at school, teasing, mimicking; but at Red Cross no one seemed to notice, she was accepted. Leaving school at 15, with no exams to her credit, she took a clerical job with Marshall's up at the aerodrome. Here her friends in the office helped her with the stutter, so that it was no longer an agony for her. Today the impediment has quite gone.

At 18 she joined the army, enlisting as a private in Queen Alexandra's Royal Army Nursing Corps, passing her S.R.N. three and a half years later. She went on to become a sergeant and then came out; but it was in the army that she discovered certain things about herself: 'I enjoyed the discipline, knowing exactly where you stood and no nonsense about it. It was a very black and white life, no vague areas of indecision. That's how I run my ward here — firmly, I'm one of them but they know where they stand.'

Sister Pargeter is in charge of the Neuro-Surgical ward, dealing with brain damage, tumours. She moves about the ward confidently; you know who is boss. 'This old gentleman,' she says, in the door of an intensive care unit, 'has been very poorly. Oh dear, we nicked his chin shaving him this morning.' Intuitively, she reaches out to touch his face, to be of comfort. 'We overlook fields here. Country people like that ... they miss the green and the trees. You have to be particularly gentle with some of these cases. For brain operations, you see, their heads are shaved. It's a nasty shock, particularly to a woman, to see herself for the first time. We help with wigs, but you've somehow got to be more considerate. The fact that I'm so ordinary, coming from such an ordinary background is a help here ... they're ordinary themselves and they see that I'm one of them. It helps them talk to me, to trust me.'

Away from the ward she relaxes in the deserted

Sisters' Room. It is an anonymous room, with bright yellow wallpaper, institution furniture; it is windowless. There is a constant throb of air-conditioning, giving an impression that one is aboard ship. Kay Pargeter seems to find the anonymity welcoming; as though she would consider more luxurious surroundings superfluous. Talking about herself is obviously a novel experience; she weighs each word at first, fearful of giving wrong measure; as she becomes less self-conscious, sentences thread together until the flow becomes almost cathartic. There is an innocent quality about her, nothing devious. She is part puritan, part ingénue. It is as if no one has ever been interested enough to ask her about herself.

'I don't find it easy to make friends — even with the other sisters. The young ones have their boy friends . . . a lot of the older ones are unmarried like me, but they have their interests. We have quite a lot of parties here, but I'm not very good at them — it's all right when I'm helping, serving drinks and so on, but I couldn't go up to a group of people and say "I'm Kay Pargeter" . . . I'm no good at small talk. I don't like going without a partner — and I haven't got one.

'I'm a very good aunty to my sisters' children. We're all close as a family. I live at home with my mother, she's a marvellous mum, does my washing . . . father was killed five years ago, you see, knocked off his bicycle by a car driven by an ex-patient of mine. Ironic, isn't it? I went through a bad patch then. People don't seem able to grieve properly — you should be able to have a good cry. It's this "model living", to put a brave front on. I couldn't cry because my brothers were abroad and I had to pull the family through.

'But I'm amazed at how brave patients are. East Anglians hate to be a bother, and they never treat me other than as a special person in the wards. Country people are stronger, they're real workers still, and they look after their elderly, visit the sick much more than city people. I know some urban families who have literally sold off parents' possessions the moment the old folk are admitted to hospital — they feel they've got rid of them. Country people are more used to death as well . . . they're brought up with it in nature. It's all around them, in the woods and fields. They have a respect for death, but less fear.

'I don't think I could cope with knowing I only had a few months to live, so I don't think we should tell patients until a fairly advanced stage. It's not good, surely, to take away hope? There are exceptions . . . like with a very close couple. Mostly they don't want to know, they steer round it — almost as if they want to protect us from the wretched job of telling them.

'There's not the practical faith today. My grandmother died at 80 of liver cancer. She'd lost three children from diphtheria and she was looking forward to seeing them again. She knew when she was going, so she called the family in, said goodbye to them and drifted off quite happily. I don't have that faith and I don't go to church. I don't think I could altogether believe in God, seeing as much suffering as I do. It can be a crutch to some people . . . and I've heard some strange stories from patients who've been resuscitated. There was one man who swore he'd been to another world and was pulled back here.'

After her eight hours' shift at Addenbrooke's, Kay changes from nursing uniform into the uniform of an officer in the Q.A.R.A.N.C., Sister Pargeter becomes Captain Pargeter. She sets out for Norwich to join her territorial army unit. She admits that a uniform gives her reassurance, endorses her identity. Out of uniform she feels like a displaced person.

'In the service, in uniform, there's a ready-made social life. Usually I don't get asked to many unofficial parties — because I'm alone and they probably think I'm too serious. Which is why I like talking to old people and Norfolk people — they mean what they say. I suppose I'm shy with men. There was someone I liked once . . .

'Perhaps I'm afraid of being hurt. I put the clamps on and my guard comes up. I'm very old-fashioned — no, I wouldn't like to be a young girl now, there's too much going on. I remember being terribly shocked when I heard that a couple were living together without being married. I worry about children — they're of another age — and with all their qualifications are they getting anything from life? I wish I had a better brain, but I've come to terms with my limitations. We learnt a lot from those old battle-axes on the wards . . . they set high standards. The standards are being kept in nursing, even improved, and I'm happy about that; but I'm not so sure about other things.

'Perhaps I get too involved. At one stage I couldn't sleep, couldn't switch off. Now I accept that if it's time to go off duty, off I go — to the Territorials or to the Dramatic Society. Oh, not on stage . . . nothing would drag me on to the stage, but I'll do any other job. I'm surer of myself that way, not out of depth. Like nursing — I know where I stand — but if I have to write a letter I'll do it two or three times.'

She screws up her brow at the thought. She has an immobile face; she doesn't give much away. It is impossible to imagine her swearing or throwing a teapot at someone. Her smiles are hesitant, rare. She says that she was nervous at the thought of talking like this — she asked her mother if she thought she should — but that it hasn't been so bad at all.

'No, I'm not a frivolous person.' She considers the proposition earnestly for a moment. 'And I'm quite trusting in some ways, not tough . . . it's just that I've been had a couple of times. I've just bought this car, a three years old Ford Capri. I didn't have it properly checked or anything, just signed the papers. Will it be all right, do you think?

'I suppose at 38 I should have made Nursing Officer grade by now, be in a more administrative position. Of course I should care about the future, but I had such an ordinary start . . . it's still a bit of a marvel being a nurse.'

The Weekenders: Adam and Juliet Sandys

EVERY FRIDAY afternoon Adam and Juliet Sandys close the door of their Chelsea house, turn their car into King's Road and head towards East Anglia. Two and a half hours later they pull up on the gravel driveway of Chelton Old Rectory, a rather isolated spot in the hinterland between Stowmarket and Diss. At six o'clock on Monday morning they motor back to London.

The Old Rectory, built in 1826, stands in three acres of matured garden. There are island beds, rare shrubs, a lawn smooth as billiard baize, not a weed in sight. There is a walled vegetable garden, growing produce for the Sandys' needs both here and in London. The modern swimming pool is secluded, out of sight of the house. A gardener comes several days a week.

Clematis and wistaria climb up the house in which there are six bedrooms, four bathrooms. The drawing room is 36 feet long, the dining room slightly smaller. On a June Sunday morning Mozart comes from a stereophonic system in the drawing room, music filling the house. Breakfast things are on the table, *The Observer* and *Sunday Times* pages scattered. Adam is wearing a yellow T-shirt with 'I love Linda Lovelace' on the chest; Juliet wears a bikini. She, at 28, has a part-time job as a secretary. Adam, who is 36, is a banker. They have no children.

'I was at the University of East Anglia,' says Juliet, 'and came to love the area. So when we started looking for a weekend place, I aimed in this direction and Adam went along with me. We looked at about 30 houses, driving out from London each weekend, but the moment we saw the hall and staircase here we just said, "Ah, isn't it lovely," and fell for it. We bought it from a millionaire, having to complete within a certain time so that he could save £30,000 in tax. The décor was hideous; but structurally it was perfect. It seemed very natural to me... I was brought up in a similar house, mummy was queen bee of the W.I., we had a full-time gardener, I went to pony club . . . really I was type-cast for this sort of background.

'When we arrived we were solemnly introduced to the daily and her husband, but that didn't work out. He was just too humble, too subservient, virtually touching his forelock as if he was willing me to play the lady of the manor. He was hopeless in the garden, trading on our own inexperience . . . and he stole booze. Mrs. Grace we have now is marvellous. She is that rare creature, a non-gossiper — she never tells me about other people, which makes me think she doesn't tell them about us.

'The local builder was splendid as well . . . we couldn't bear to waste our weekends painting. But every now and then they'd down tools and rush off . . . we couldn't understand why until we learned that they were undertakers as well. On their writing paper they have "Builders" in plain script, then "Funeral Directors" in huge black gothic.

'By and large we found reaction a mixture of helpfulness and curiosity — and of course tradesmen saying they'd do something and you'd wait ages and ages and keep chasing; but it's exactly the same in London. The local "gentry" were also curious. They had drinks parties so that we could meet the neighbours and when they said, "You must come to dinner," they actually followed it up, which is pretty unusual. Our first summer we spent two weeks' holiday here and dined out 10 times — but I think they were surprised to find us so young.'

Adam is in the garden, adjusting a hose. He returns to the terrace, pours a glass of grapefruit juice. He is taciturn, using words economically; his look is of part-amusement, part-boredom. He has a semi-detached way about him. He yawns a lot.

'We haven't been here long enough to have firm opinions. There's no real village here, you can't go and have a pint with the locals; but society appears very stratified compared with Yorkshire where I was brought up. There's an *Akenfield* hangover of bitterness between landowner and landless; nor are there any great families nearby around which life revolves.

'Our nearest neighbour is a farmer, we call him "Fagin". He's about 70, first generation to own his land — about 60 acres and he'd be better off drawing the old age pension. His tractor's 20 years old and during the harvest his antique combine bursts into flames — we helped him put the fire out last summer. He's suspicious, narrow-minded... thought we were a bit of a joke at first — until he saw our cabbages grow bigger than his. He's earthy — but when we moved in he came over and said he wanted to be a good neighbour.'

Juliet: 'I think he quite fancies my bikini. It was a bit chilly after a heatwave and he said to me, "Well, you won't be wearing that by-keeny today then". There was talk about how shocked they were by nude bathing, but to see anyone in the pool you'd need to be up a very tall tree with a very strong telescope...

'Down here we tend to work all day in the garden, and we eat well — I buy meat in the village and bring food from London I can't get here, like fish and cheese. We have house-parties in summer which usually means a dinner party for 10 or 12 on Saturday evening. We tend not to get involved with village life, fêtes and so on. We go to church on high days and holidays — there's a regular elderly congregation of about 12 — and I do the winter flowers occasionally when you have to buy them. The form is that people from the cottages do them in summer when you can pick them.'

Adam: 'No, we don't go to the Aldeburgh Festival. We would if it wasn't so dominated by Britten's music and Pears' voice. We go to musical evenings at Kentwell Hall and Olga Ironside-Woods' play in Ipswich... usually we plan these outings for our guests, not if we're alone. In London we go to the opera and Juliet goes to most major exhibitions — she keeps me in touch because I'm usually working until eight o'clock. The main object here is to recuperate from London and to pursue our interest in growing things. I see enough of people in London — the decision makers. I find it more difficult to adapt from the country to London than vice versa.

'But if we wanted to live the whole time in the country, it couldn't be here. Why? Well, you can't walk for one thing — we're in the heart of the country but if we want to walk we have to get in the car to drive somewhere. It's all arable. Another thing — the wind pattern has changed since we came. It used to be from the west, now it's from the north, so we hear traffic from that dual-carriageway. Aeroplanes too... it's a good place on balance, but only for weekends.'

They move from the terrace to the pool where Adam methodically tests the chlorine content, balancing solutions in test tubes, holding them to the light. He reads the temperature. Juliet slips into the water, unconcerned by the chill; she swims a few lengths' breast stroke before sitting on the edge, dangling her legs over the side. She shakes her hair: 'I've no pet hates, but people here aren't remotely concerned with any of the larger issues of life . . . it's as if there's an Idi Amin fan club, everyone thoroughly unliberal, totally, exclusively concerned with the comfortable, narrow lives they lead. And my blood boils about the trees and hedges . . .'

Adam: 'I intensely dislike the local farmers' attitude to trees and hedgerows. It's boorish — it's strange being so close to London that they're such an isolated people. Parochialism I admire provided it's tempered with pride, but they're so destructive — all they want is 100 acre fields. And the Suffolk County Council is the most philistinic I've come across — in Lincolnshire for instance they plant millions of trees, in Suffolk they scarcely plant any. The councils are inefficient, the farmers lack appreciation of the countryside's beauty.

'I wanted to plant trees myself along the road — I tried the council but soon gave that up, then I tried the farmers . . . same result. So I went ahead and planted. What happened? A local farmer came along and cut the saplings down.

'It's much the same with building development. There are the Chelsworths and the Lavenhams where it's been handled with admirable restraint, but the ribbon development of most villages is appalling. You'll never see the same in Oxfordshire or Gloucestershire — where they use local material, Cotswold stone . . .

'Yet I suppose there's something reassuring in this East Anglian obstinacy, the way it refuses to be drawn into the stresses and fashions of the times. It goes its own way.'

Chelton Old Rectory has a fine staircase and fine wines; the clematis has taken perfectly, furniture glows under care. The Sandys enjoy their Mozart and their swimming pool and the peace of a beautiful house and garden . . . from Friday evening until the dawn of Monday. Then the house stands empty, its burglar alarm primed to discourage trespassers. It becomes a home unlived in, echoing only to memories of times past. No doubt it is much loved, on a part time basis; its master and mistress are in transit. It would not suit all of us; we would become disoriented, time here and time there confusing us. Perhaps we have not grasped relativity in the way of a man who plants trees, who understands that

Time present and time past
Are both perhaps present in time future,
And time future contained in time past.

Adam: 'Sometimes it's awful to go back to London, but it would be equally awful not to go. Our aim has never been to become deeply rooted into the community... we're weekenders.'

The School Leaver: Sandy Winterton

'I DON'T HAVE many friends at school — just a few I have things in common with; I can get on with them. I don't really like most people — they're boring. Most of them at school know what they're going to do, most of them are trying for university . . . everyone will go to university in a few years' time, and can you see there being enough jobs for all those graduates?

'I've no idea what I want to do, I honestly haven't. And I've no idea why I'm like this — I've had encouragement from my parents, from the careers master. All I'm sure of is that I've got to get away, to have a rest . . . I feel as if I've been over-educated, run through a sausage machine, and now I want to get away. Not to university, at least not yet — I'll leave my options open about that.

'I like open spaces. I'm a great ornithologist, naturalist . . . we're in suburbia here, but you can be on Rushmere Heath in a few minutes. The freedom of an acre and a cow appeals to me, but they won't let you do it, the System is against it. They want you to conform, that's the state of the world's politics . . . producing everyone to be the same, and it's the biggest crime there could be. I loathe socialism for this reason — I'd vote conservative, except that I can't take Maggie Thatcher . . . that voice, she's a child, always knocking holes in other ideas but not building new ones of her own. She's dragging the conservatives down.'

Sandy Winterton is 18 years old, about to take 'A' levels before leaving Northgate School in Ipswich at the end of term. He lives with his parents in their semi-detached in Brunswick Road. There is a mass of flowers in the minute front garden. The sitting room has a divan sofa, two chairs, colour television; a whole tortoise shell hangs on the wall near a painting of Pin Mill. There are other paintings, badly drawn, but alive; someone has made a choice away from safe classical prints. There are few books, *The Life and Times of Chopin, Flower Arranging* and *House Plants, Which?* the *Sunday Times Magazine.* Despite the pictures, it is an unemphatic room, neither welcoming nor unwelcoming. It reminds one of a dentist's waiting room.

Sandy is a good looking young man, tall and strongly built. He is very direct, looking at you directly. He is not shy and he is not arrogant; he is relaxed, at ease and interested. He is tired, having just returned from a few days' camping. He is smoking, his long legs stretched before him. He has no trouble with words, stringing them together fluidly, unselfconsciously, without trying to be clever.

'I went to kindergarten at four, but can't remember much of that — then to Sidegate Primary from four to eight. It was adding, subtracting, the alphabet, playing with plasticine and bricks . . . yes, the teachers were fine, nice people — but it came as a bump to move up. Suddenly things got complicated, we were expected to learn — history, geography, science. That was in the Junior School and the teachers didn't seem to be on our side . . . in the infants' we couldn't get into trouble, but now we could be punished, stood in the corner. There was one teacher, a real "old school tie" character who literally always wore his school tie and blazer . . . I loathed him because he was inadequate as a teacher.

'One day, with no warning, we were taken into the hall, sat at desks and given exam papers to answer — English, Maths, General Knowledge. Two months passed and then a letter came to say I'd got through and would be going to Northgate. Then another letter came from the school saying I would need two pairs of rugby shorts, house colours, a pair of this and two pairs of that. And I was given a house, Tempest House — sounds like public school but it wasn't, the house was really just for sports. Yes, my parents knew all about the cost because of my two brothers and sister who'd done the same before me. I'd done well, but no one told me how well, I was in the dark about that — if I'd failed I'd have gone to Copplestone Road Comprehensive School.

'Northgate was another bump in a way — I thought the buildings were horrible, so big and foreboding. Bells rang every 40 minutes and we'd get lost looking for classrooms for the next period . . . there were 50 classrooms.

There were two buildings, one for boys and one for girls, with complete segregation then — about 1,500 of us in all. Today it's about 2,000. Eventually we went comprehensive and girls mixed in with boys . . . no, I don't think this was a good thing because the girls' teachers were pretty old and strict, very few of them married — they stood for established tradition, not looking to the future. The boys had more freedom and the teachers were basically good.

'We didn't make special allowances for the girls, and they didn't seem to expect it — it's just that they seemed less *interested*. I was always asking questions, asking and asking until I really understood, but the girls just took it in parrot fashion without grasping the meaning at all. They passed exams all right, but it meant nothing to them, they'd recited facts.

'Science runs in the family, to degree level . . . I'd started at 11 with a chemistry set — I started experimenting. That's what I was interested in, but I was doing art, German, French, Latin, divinity . . . I couldn't understand why a boy who wanted to become a metal worker should spend so much time on Shakespeare, or why someone who wanted to learn a Common Market language should take Latin, a dead language. But I got all my 'O' levels except German which I took again in the sixth form and passed. About 80% stayed on, the rest went to Civic College or into jobs. I wanted to leave, I was fed up with being educated, but I was persuaded . . . it was the argument of the short term versus the long term.

'Anyway, there's been far more freedom in the sixth form, we do much as we want and I specialise in biology and physics . . . then there's games or community work. But I don't think I shall do well over 'A' levels; I've hardly revised at all. I really *don't* care about university — I'm just fed up with education. The moment term is over I'm going to Wales to a job as a canoe instructor at an Adventure Centre on the River Wye. They'll pay me £7 a week, that's all . . . but money doesn't interest me much, I don't need it — I just need to get away, I keep saying that I know, but I feel stifled. I haven't been getting on with my parents lately either . . . they'll be happy if I get a job so that I can leave home. There's friction.

'No, I'm not disillusioned. It's an efficient machine for processing people to university — this is the ideal really, a manufacturing process for producing average human beings, average well-read people. I'm just saying that it could have been more exciting, the teachers could have been more inspired . . . they're good, they're decent people, it's just that there's no inspiration. But it's helped me understand what makes people tick — there are a lot of opportunities to meet people with varying interests. There are school clubs for almost everything — chess, bridge, drama — anyone can go to the Head and be given encouragement to start a new club.

'Equality? We shouldn't grumble about that. Some public schoolboys look on us as plebs, and it doesn't worry me at all — any more than their "old boy network" which may get them better jobs. There must be differences — it's a fact of life and it would be boring otherwise. There's nothing wrong in having a Public School System — what would be wrong is that there should be no choice.'

The educational processing plant has failed to stamp a serial number on Sandy Winterton. Like an export reject, he does not bear the manufacturer's seal of serviceability. 'I've no idea what I want to do, I honestly haven't,' he has said. But at least he knows what he does not want to do: he does not want to go to Oxbridge, he does not want to vote socialist, equally he does not want to vote for Margaret Thatcher. Somewhere along the line, something has gone wrong: the process has hiccupped, assembling an individual. Whether by accident or industrial espionage, the machinery is imperfect and we should thank God that it is so.

Time is on Sandy's side. At school he asks questions, asking and asking until he really understands. The important questions have still to be answered. Canoeing on the River Wye may answer one or two . . . and then?

'I must have open space. I'll go to France — there's more room there, and then I'll head for Spain. That's as far as I can think at the moment. The System is behind me . . . you've got to be smart enough to take it as far as it goes, but no further.'

One fine morning Sandy will set off, leaving his country behind him. He is a sensitive person, full of intelligence and good intent. If he does not return, the loss will be ours.

The Baker: Ian Kelly

BRAMPTON has never really set the world on fire. Its sons have included no Cokes, no Nelsons, no Wolseys. Its pace has always been that of the Sabbath day, a gentle step; yet there is a quality about the place . . .
    'And a child that's born on the Sabbath day
    Is fair and wise and good and gay.'
Perhaps Brampton was born on the Sabbath. There is no knowing, of course. All we know is that the land was held in Saxon times by Padda, and that by the time of the compilation of Domesday it was held by Robert de Curcande, as part of the vast possessions granted to Roger, Earl of Bigod. The manor comprised two carucates (about 240 acres) with two villeins and six bordars (smallholders) held in demesne or farmed directly.

God arrived formally in Brampton in the person of His servant, Augustus fil Aug. de la Cliff, de Donewico, in 1323, to be appointed first Rector of St. Peter's Church. There was a bit of a lull after that; not much excitement, you could say, until the Victorian era. Steam came to Brampton then, and this was positively epoch-making, for although the railway line cut the parish in half and the station is a long walk from anywhere of population, it was — and still is — an asset shared by few other small villages.

The best known name hereabouts is Leman; it was Sir John who became lord and patron in 1606 when he was Sheriff of London. Later he became Lord Mayor of the City, dying in 1632 to be buried, far from home, in the Fishmongers' Chapel, Crooked Lane, in the City. The Lemans continued to hold the manor and advowson until 1807, when Mary Leman rather let the side down by electing to remain a spinster, the property passing after her death to her near relation, the Reverend Naunton Thomas Orgill. He assumed the name and arms of Leman by royal licence and built Brampton Hall c.1794 where, either through a sense of responsibility to restore the *status quo* or purely through self-indulgence, he proceeded to sire 12 children. The Hall stands today, red-brick and masterful, but the Lemans have gone their way.

Not far from the imposing Hall, on the corner, is an imposing sign. So eye-catching is it that one quite expects a proclamation of the sort that Brampton is twinned with Château Bourganeuf in Clermont Ferrand. But no, 'BRAMPTON VILLAGE BAKERY', reads the sign in huge red characters; an arrow points brazenly towards The Street. It should not be there at all: you should apply for planning permission, licences, court orders, to do a thing like that. But it all takes months and months and months, and everyone is dead or moved to Bungay by the time approval comes through. So there it is — BRAMPTON VILLAGE BAKERY. Sometime a chap from the Ministry will come along and order its removal; until then we all know where to buy better bread.

Brampton Village Stores and Bakery is a low white cottage, huddled on to the lane. It was built about 150 years ago and whoever laid the floors must have been awfully drunk at the time. The Stores sell Vicks Vapour Rub and Shredded Wheat, Maltesers and tinned peaches, Veno's Cough Syrup and Golden Syrup, fly killer, Player's Weights, birthday cards and mousetraps. The door makes little tinging noises as villagers come in, armed with string bags and horrifying accounts of their infirmities: 'Hello, Pat love, I'll have two lemon curd tarts, a sausage roll for tea, a book of matches . . . and-did-you-know-I-didn't-get-a-wink-of-sleep-until-4 o'clock-this-morning-until-I-took-the-pills-for-my-back-it-was-hurting-something-dreadful-it's-right-down-low-about-here-dear-do-you-see . . .'. And Pat Kelly says yes, how painful it must be, as she wraps the lemon curd tarts, the sausage roll and replies for the 23rd time that morning that it's nice to see the sun at last.

But customers do not drive all the way from Norwich, Lowestoft, Beccles, Southwold, for Golden Syrup, or even for Pat's meteorological observations. They come for bread: large square crusty whites, curly brown granary loaves, long sticks of French bread — baked behind the shop and left to cool, spreading tantalizing aromas into the Suffolk air. It is a reassuring smell, spanning the years at a single sniff to those days when the world was young and we were less sophisticated in our demand for loaves that are pre-sliced, pre-wrapped, mass-manufactured to a texture of tightly knitted socks.

'Baking's in my blood,' says Ian Kelly. 'Mother came from Switzerland and her three brothers, my uncles, are all master bakers in Basle. I used to go and watch them at work when I was a child . . . yes, it's in my blood all right, I just never wanted to do anything else. I've got a feeling for bread. Dough's good to handle . . . you *mould* it into shape and you know you're producing something good, something of quality.'

Baking, to Ian Kelly, is a vocation; he has been Called to the Oven. The Maid of Orleans heard voices; Ian Kelly heard them too: 'Dough,' they murmured — and so to the staff of life he devotes himself.

Ian may have this special feeling for bread, but the melancholy fact remains that his passion is not entirely reciprocated. Not to put too fine a point on it, Ian Kelly is allergic to flour.

'I was working for my City and Guilds when it first came on. I started to get this wheeze on the chest. I sneezed a lot and my eyes went red every time I went near flour. The doctors didn't cure it, so they said I must give up baking. Well, I didn't know what to do. I mean, I couldn't give it up. You can't, can you? So I went to Eastaugh's, the family baker in Bungay . . . but it got worse, the flour gave me conjunctivitis. It got so bad I had to leave . . . I took a job with a big poultry group at Flixton as a band-sawman, cutting up frozen chicken. I hated it, felt like a machine — but there was the mortgage to meet. We even had to ask permission to go to the toilet. That embarrassed me because my charge hand was a lady . . . but I used to talk to them about bread and they asked me to make some for them in my spare time. I ended up baking 40 loaves a week for the staff at that poultry place . . .

'I couldn't stay away from baking for long. I had to return to bread . . . then we heard about The Stores, so we came here. I can manage with this nasal spray and I have S.D.V. injections; but my eyes still swell up like balloons if I get a grain of flour in them. Baking's not very rewarding financially, the reward's in the satisfaction, doing what I enjoy . . . it *must* be born in me. I don't get much time for anything else.'

The Kelly's sitting room is between the shop and the

bakery. There is a picture of Vesuvius erupting and, because Ian is interested in the martial arts, a photograph of Bruce Lee. Cartons of Heinz, and Walker's cheese and onion flavoured crisps pile one on top of the other, almost ceiling high. They share the room with two children, a Collie called Lady and a cat, Pooh. The telephone keeps ringing and Pat answers, taking down orders for small whites, half a dozen rolls. Ian gets up every few moments to see if his oven is still there.

'Factory bread? It's all right . . . . it's all water really, isn't it? About 90% water . . . it's conveyor-belt baking. I only use the best flour, and the best fat, salt and yeast. I mix the dough, two stone of flour gives me 80 lbs of dough, about 40 loaves. My mixer does it in five minutes — it stands for about half an hour then until it doubles in size, the yeast swelling. Then I scale it off to size, hand it up into balls and let it stand for another five minutes before moulding it into tins until the yeast rises to the top of each tin. Lay the tins in the oven next, pushing it in with this "peel". It bakes for 20 minutes at 450° to 500°, and then for the last 20 minutes at 420° so it doesn't burn. You know if the bread is cooked by tapping the bottom of the loaf . . . if it makes this hollow sound, it's done.'

Ian, who is 27, works a minimum 14 hours a day, usually starting at 4 a.m. On Saturday he starts at 1 a.m. He smiles wryly at the editorial comment in his trade magazine, *British Baker:* 'Already we are hearing of bakeries wanting to introduce 12-hour shifts . . . that's far too many hours to work.' He produces an average 80 loaves a day, but increases to 200 to meet special weekend demand. He still has a very long way to go to make the big time: Tooks of Ipswich bake 420,000 loaves a week, about 70,000 each day.

Ian Kelly is not much interested in expansion: 'If you do that then there's no money; you're always owing the bank. I'm independent like this . . .' He loses the thread; baking is my job, seems to be his sentiment, not business: 'People live off bread, for breakfast, dinner and tea. Baking's coming back in, it's not a dying trade. You can't say that about many, can you?'

His wife, Pat, is the go-ahead one: 'I'm the business partner; I'd like to expand, to take a shop in a thoroughfare, like Tooks. I wouldn't push Ian — if he's happy, I'm happy. But it makes me think . . . we never have a loaf left at the end of the day, and every one is ordered. Often we have none left for the family . . . we could sell so much more.'

They are talking about a new oven, one which will hold two trays and take up a lot more space; but it all means planning permission and rebuilding and a thousand miles of red tape. It would increase output tremendously, producing 200 loaves a baking instead of the present 40; yet Ian does not give the impression that his heart is entirely in it. He is a kind of Rembrandt, reluctantly considering group portraiture.

His message is evangelical: 'There are some youngsters who have never tasted real bread . . .'. This troubles him; he reaches, frowning, for his nasal spray. 'It's depriving old folk as well . . . there's this saying you hear, "best thing since sliced bread". Well, that's pretty daft, isn't it? There's an old boy out at Woodside old people's home — he said to me my bread was the only real bread he's tasted in 50 years. He said my bread was a Godsend. That's what he said, a Godsend. Now that's what I call my reward.'

The Gravedigger: Amos Legge

'I'VE BEEN a devil in my time,' Amos Legge announces proudly. He rubs his grizzled head, looking baffled but not at all contrite. 'God's a marvellous man . . . I uphold his views in every way. But all the rest are buggers. Snobbish too. Everyone's a snob today. They won't talk to you unless they're after something. They're all newcomers too — don't belong here. All the old ones have gone, moved away or died. I should know . . . buried most of 'em myself. I've buried thousands, *thousands.*'

Deersthorpe is 20 miles from King's Lynn, pressed in by the weight of surrounding agriculture in a way that a collector's wildflower is squashed between the pages of a book. The sap has been squeezed out of Deersthorpe, replaced by thinner stuff, etiolated city blood retired to modernised cottages called Sycamore View and Dunroamin. Television aerials take root among the thatch; net curtains, like gauze bandages, give the place an antiseptic look. Men polish Rover 2000's, and invite the golf club secretary home for gin and tonic.

When Amos emerges from his cottage, which is rare enough these days unless he has a job on, he hates what he sees. His hatred is savage; it is as if he is scheming his own gunpowder plot on Dunroamin. 'Buggers,' he says, tearing, quite literally, at his hair.

Amos Legge's cottage faces on to the lane, partly screened by an untrimmed, unruly hedge. One wall is white, the next pink, as if the decorator simply used up whatever paint was handy, unconcerned by Ideal Home hints for colour scheme. Sheets of corrugated metal lie in the garden, together with oil drums, netting, a collection of weather vanes. There is a cold tap — the only source of water — and a couple of huts, one of which contains the lavatory.

The front room, which few people have been privileged to see, is said to contain huge quantities of bird seed. Upstairs is Amos' bedroom. There is no bathroom.

Amos spends most of his waking hours in a downstairs room, once the kitchen, about nine feet long by five across. A crucifix is suspended above a bird cage containing four budgies: 'That's George, and that one answers to Blue Boy. The others don't have names. They all used to talk from morning 'til night, then one little fellow died. Lay there he did with his little feet in the air, and they all stopped talking to this day. I think they were grieving with me. They twitter all the time, 'specially when someone comes, it's just that they don't talk sensibly as they used to. Whatever that bird died of was contagious. I went into hospital next day for seven weeks . . . prostate gland.'

Amos has always loved animals. As a child his hobby was making tiny coffins for pet guinea pigs, rabbits, cats. Then he would give them a decent Christian burial. He remembers dressing up once as a parson so that he could conduct a funeral service. He had no other interest. He didn't play football with the other village boys. Just made sure that dead animals were treated with proper respect.

In 1917, when he was 13 years old, he became a full time gravedigger. Apart from five years' army service in the Second World War, this has been his life work. He has been digging graves in 38 neighbouring parishes for 61 years, earning from 7s. 6d. to £4 or £5 for a grave. One undertaker pays him £12. He is a short man, only 5ft. 4ins., but with immensely broad shoulders. Shaking hands with him is a hazard; his grip could dislocate bones.

'I've got a back today. I wear a steel corset and a truss. There's a lot wrong with me these days — but I forget it all when I'm digging. Digging makes me better. My graves are neat, they fit well. It's my pride, my vocation. Rich or poor, I give them the same job. Graves are my life.

'Six foot six for a single, seven foot six a double, and nine foot for a treble grave. That's the measurements. Not that I like these family graves much . . . a woman wants to be put next to her husband when she dies a few years later, you see. Well, I have to open the grave . . . coffin's collapsed, very likely, and the body's like raw meat. Cremation's cleaner. It's against my own trade to say so, but I'll be cremated. Not that I'll have much say in the matter. They do what they want with you these days. No respect today . . . it's a modern world.

'When I dug my first grave, you could be buried for next to nothing. Good Lord, it costs £200 or so to be buried by the Co-op today, and that don't include the party afterwards. That's all people come for, the food and drink ... and to see what they've been left. Families used to mourn, really mourn. They'd put the body in the parlour for 12 days so that friends could pay their respects ... used to go off a bit in hot weather. They used to wear black mourning bands for months. Today people attend the funeral in all colours of the rainbow. And when it comes to "earth to earth, ashes to ashes, dust to dust", they don't want to know. I throw some earth down on the coffin, but they don't — they can't wait to get away to their tea and ham sandwiches. It's one bloody great picnic.

'Reminds me, there was this old fellow dying and he hadn't been allowed to eat for days. Then the doctor told his wife that the patient didn't have much time left, so she could feed him anything he fancied. After the doctor had gone the woman called up the stairs to let the dying man know he could eat what he liked. "I'd like some o' that there ham yow a'got cooken down there," replied the husband. "Yow can't hev thet," said his wife. "Thet's for the funeral."

'I've kept records of everyone I've buried since 1917, all by name. I know where they are and how I dug the grave. I miss some of 'em, but they're happier where they are. Takes me the whole day to dig a grave in clay, but I can do three a day in good ground. You put 'em in so that their feet are to the east — all except the parson. You put him in the other way round so that when he's resurrected he'll blow his trumpet facing his flock. I asked the Bishop about this once: "What happens, my lord," I said, "When they bury the parson in the middle of the graveyard?" He didn't seem to make much of that.

'There was another old fellow whose wife lay dying and she threatened that if he married again she'd "scrab" her way out of her grave to haunt him. But this old fellow did marry again, and the new parson who had heard of the curse asked the man if he wasn't frightened. "Doan't yew know," the man told the parson, "I buried owd Bessie face down, so the harder she scrab the fudder down she keep a-goin'."

'You've got to be careful burying the dead ... they

might come back, as a dog or something. There's a lot worse things you could come back as than a dog. Yes, I like working for the dead — they're the best sort. Not that the ones walking about aren't half dead. This lady said to me, didn't I worry about working in a graveyard at dusk with all the dead, and I said no, it was the buggers walking around that worried me.

'I've buried them from stillborns to well over 100 years old — buried a lady of 105 last month, fit as a fiddle she was, still living alone and looking after herself. I told you. I've buried thousands, and never had a single complaint...

'But still I'll be cremated if I get the chance. As I say, it's cleaner. Used to like the idea of being scattered on the wind, but I don't know if they allow it any more. Probably someone from the environment... he'll tell it's mucky having dead people's ash blowing all over the place. They'll have to put my ashes in a jar and bury me. Like to see how the parson works out where my head and feet are for the resurrection.'

Locally, Amos Legge is known as an irascible old man, the sort who sees good in nothing; and mostly he is given a wide berth. Perhaps too he is a little feared. When he sets off on his new Japanese motor cycle, gleaming fork and spade strapped to the carrier, it is known that he is on an errand of death. Each journey is a reminder that everyone will need his services once.

This social isolation distresses him. He admits to loneliness, particularly when he is not well. He keeps his courage up by ranting at the world in general, his face becoming suffuse as he considers the injustice of it all. But when he has huffed and puffed his fill, he suddenly subsides, looking desperately about his possessions as if they will give him substance. There are brass shell cases, a pile of O.H.M.S. buff envelopes, pipe rack (seldom is there a pipe or hand-rolled cigarette out of his mouth), faded newspaper cuttings, empty orange squash bottles. There is a photograph of him, smart in a suit and cloth cap, taken up against a headstone. Where else?

A clothes lines stretches above his head, upon which hang the shirt and underpants he has washed. He eats chips and boiled potatoes, and Meals on Wheels give him three hot dinners a week; but he says he does not need much food. Usually he is in bed by eight, and there he stays until midday or so; unless there is a grave to dig. Nothing, even double-pneumonia, would keep him from his ordained duty of preparing the ground for the dead.

'Oh, I used to have another interest. I was verger and sexton at St. Peter's. Fifty five years I never missed a service. Not one. I loved that church. Kept it tidy and clean, grass was always trimmed. Rang the bell, I did, and took the plate round. Then this new vicar came. Told me I needed help, that I was too old to do it all alone. He was really telling me I wasn't wanted. I knew how to do it. That church was spotless and I didn't need help. They just didn't want me. So I left and I've never set foot inside the church since that day.

'They aren't *real* parsons any more. They're ex-policemen or generals who've come into it and don't believe half they're paid to preach. You can't trust them . . . like women. I was married 25 years and my wife died when we moved here from the other end of the village. I dug her grave. Lived alone for three years, but couldn't stand that after a good woman, so I married again. I wanted a housekeeper, she wanted a position. We didn't love each other. She left me after a year and 10 months — hated my guts. She had other activities. Tom, Dick, and Harry. They're all flipperty these days, it's that bloody National Health business . . . give 'em all pills and they think they can do what they like. There's no such thing as a good marriage today. People have gone mad. There's nothing wrong with the world, just people have gone mad.'

Amos Legge is aggrieved. He has been done wrong; he has grown old and been rejected. He has few material comforts in life; and yet it is whispered about the village that he has saved a fortune, never spending a penny. So why won't he install a bathroom, an inside lavatory, buy an electric blanket?

'What do I want with a 'lectric blanket? I've never had one. It'd kill me. They give you shocks. Bathroom? That'd mean a grant and I'm not having them people about the place. They'd put up the rates. Once you get into their clutches . . . .' He becomes secretive, sly, yet obviously enjoying himself. 'Oh, yes, I've got a nest egg, something for a rainy day. You'd be surprised. If I die?' (He appears surprised, as if he had not thought that one day someone might have to dig his grave.) 'Well . . . I'd leave it to someone, wouldn't I?'

He is silent for a while, the only sound coming from the chirping George, Blue Boy, and two nameless budgies. He looks defiant; then his eyes cloud over and he twists his calloused hands: 'I suppose I think of dying sometimes. It's no life alone, when the only callers are undertakers. No one wants you. Then I start thinking about the funeral service . . . "Man that is born of woman hath but a short time to live, and is full of misery. He cometh up, and is cut down, like a flower; he fleeth as it were a shadow, and never continueth in one stay." A bit morbid, isn't it? I'd rather have the one from Revelations, that's what I think about — "And I saw a new heaven and a new earth . . ." '

His expression changes back to defiance. He is better at being defiant. It is his anger that keeps him out of the grave: 'I've got no horror of funerals. I delight in them. I wish there was more dying. I'd rather go to a funeral than a wedding. When I go to a funeral I think to myself, it's all over, they're at peace; but when I go to a wedding I think, poor buggers, their troubles are just beginning.'